This book is dedicated to Stately Homes, their owners and their visitors, without whom the rich tapestry of Britain would be much poorer

Stately Secrets

Stately Secrets

*Behind-the-scenes stories from the
Stately Homes of Britain*

Richard, Earl of Bradford

Robson Books

This Robson paperback edition first published in 1996
First published in Great Britain in 1994 by Robson Books Ltd,
Bolsover House, 5-6 Clipstone Street, London W1P 8LE

British Library Cataloguing in Publication Data
A catalogue record for this title is available from the British Library

ISBN 0 86051 917 1 (hbk)
    1 86105 035 6 (pbk)

Printed in Great Britain by WBC Book Manufacturers Ltd., Bridgend, Mid-Glamorgan

Contents

Acknowledgements   1

Introduction   5

Mistaken Identities   11

The Doings of M'Lords   43

Staff   93

That's Entertainment   119

Sporting Chance   145

Guests (paying and otherwise)   167

Acknowledgements

Foremost I would like to thank my godson Edward Meynell for his help in compiling and writing this book. I have not been the best of godfathers, having not seen him for twenty-one years between his christening and his grandmother's funeral in autumn 1993.

His sense of humour and command of English have added immensely to the quality of this book, whilst his cheerful presence has spurred me on whenever we became slightly bogged down or had computer problems. The volume of my cellar does appear to have declined considerably during this time, but then it has been thirsty work!

A particular thank you to Harry Northumberland (The Duke of Northumberland), Lucy Sapte and all the staff at Alnwick, Syon and Albury. They entered into the spirit of the book and produced a wealth of wonderful stories.

All eight members of the Treasure Houses of England: Robin Tavistock (The Marquess of Tavistock), his secretary, Cilla Pumfrey and the staff at Woburn Abbey; The Duke of Devonshire and the Administrator, Eric Oliver, Chatsworth; George Harewood (The Earl of Harewood) and the staff, Harewood House; The Duke of Marlborough and Paul Duffie, Blenheim Palace; Mr Ralph Armond, Warwick Castle; The Hon. Simon and Mrs Howard, Castle Howard; Edward Montagu (Lord Montagu of Beaulieu) and Mrs Jill

1

Lindemere, Beaulieu; and Lord Romsey, Broadlands.

Charles Clive-Ponsonby-Fane sent me a copy of his book, *We Started a Stately Home*, together with a wealth of anecdotes, both from himself and others. Chryssie Lytton Cobbold (Lady Cobbold) of Knebworth House presented me with her publication, *Board Meetings in the Bath*. John Hoy at Knebworth also contributed.

Norman Hudson allowed us to use descriptions of stately homes from *Hudson's Historic House Directory*, whilst Terry Empson of The Historic Houses Association encouraged members to send me stories.

Finally many thanks to: Gyles Brandreth, MP; the late Bob Payton of Stapleford Park; Patrick Lichfield (The Earl of Lichfield) and Penny Daly; Cdr Michael Saunders Watson, Rockingham Castle; Sir Thomas Ingilby, Bt, Ripley Castle; Robin Bridgeman (The Viscount Bridgeman); The Earl of Carlisle, Naworth Castle; Julian Luttrell; Derek Nimmo; Other Plymouth (The Earl of Plymouth); The Duke of Wellington and Mr P. Aubrey-Fletcher, Stratfield Saye; The Duke of Richmond and Gordon, The Earl of March and the staff at Goodwood; Shaun Normanton (The Earl of Normanton), Somerley; Charlie Shelburne (The Earl of Shelburne) and Mrs Jane Meadows at Bowood; Janey Compton (Mrs Robin Compton), Newby Hall; Alexander Thynn (The Marquess of Bath), Mrs C. Everard and all at Longleat; Eiler Hansen at Berkeley Castle; The Viscount Massereene and Ferrard; Sir Westrow Hulse, Bt, Breamore; Mr T.B. Ronnay, the Administrator at Holkham Hall; The Marquess of Cholmondeley, Houghton Hall; Somerset de Chair, St Osyth's Priory; Charles Shrewsbury (The Earl of Shrewsbury); Charlie Shuttleworth (The Lord Shuttleworth); John and Jennie Makepeace, Parnham; James and Jean Starkie, Gaulden Manor; The Lady Ashcombe, Sudeley Castle; The Hon. Michael Flower, Arley Hall; Noel Boxall, Bickleigh Castle; Bunny Maitland-Carew (The Hon. Gerald

Maitland-Carew), Thirlestane Castle; Sir Reresby Sitwell, Bt, Renishaw Hall; Hugh Hertford (The Marquess of Hertford), Ragley Hall; Charlie and Maggie Wyvill, Constable Burton; The Hon. Ian Bennet, Chillingham; Mark Roper, Forde Abbey; James Hervey-Bathurst, Eastnor Castle; Ivor Spencer; Mr George Drye, Lamport Hall; David Lowsley-Williams, Chavenage; Sir Nicholas Fairbairn, QC, MP; Mrs Thea Randall at the Staffordshire Record Office; Richard Mountgarret (The Viscount Mountgarret); Sir Charles Wolseley, Bt; The Earl and Countess of Rosebery, Dalmeny House; The Viscount Norwich; Morys Aberdare (The Lord Aberdare); Lady Victoria Leatham, Burghley House, and many others who sent us contributions that owing to lack of space we were unable to include.

They have all been most patient and helpful, despite being harried and chased by me, even forced to sign disclaimer letters; however, without them this book would not have contained the wealth of new and amusing stories that we have uncovered. I hope that you enjoy reading it as much as I enjoyed writing it.

Bradford

Introduction

The purpose of this book is to take an affectionate look at the day-to-day business of stately homes – their visitors as well as their staff and owners. It is not a serious sociological study, nor is it meant to be in any way patronizing – proprietors make as many silly slips and gaffes as anyone else, as you will see. Instead it has been written as light-hearted entertainment, poking fun at all sides, and in all the dusty corners.

Britain needs stately homes that are lived in by families, preferably the descendants of their creators. Without them, the whole country could only boast, at best, a collection of sterile museum-style buildings, houses that have lost their heart and soul.

Equally, there is no way these homes will survive without the continued interest and generosity of the visiting public, or the companies that hold conferences and social events in them. They are the lifeblood of historic houses, keeping the bailiffs at bay, and providing much entertainment, amusement and insight on the way.

This humorous collection also takes a peek at the complicated world of titles and the peerage. Again, the intention is not so much to instruct as to divert. Many of the stories throughout the book come from the protagonists themselves, and combine elements of self-mockery and exasperation. Once your name has been misspelt or completely reinterpreted a thousand times, you have good reason to be a little piqued. Most of all though, you begin to appreciate the originality and imagination behind some of the more improbable renderings. I would like to think that this book catches an element of that absurdity which marks the lives and lifestyles of all involved in the world of stately homes.

When we have referred to the visitors – their comments and their actions – we have been conscious of a tendency to sound superior, as though in some way belittling them. To a great extent this is unavoidable, as it is not possible to be at once amusing and unfailingly delicate. But you may understand from a perusal of the book that, nine times out of ten, the owners come in for as much stick, and are equally, if not more so, lampooned. The humour of stately homes involves all, from butlers to baronets, and it would not be fair to spare the visiting public from similar satirical coverage.

My personal theory is that the public don't actually visit historic houses to gaze in reverence at priceless works of art, or to marvel at the splendours of antique furniture. What they really want is to look through the stately keyhole, and learn about a different way of life. They are certainly far more interested in anything that is personal, even scandalous, than that which is merely artistic or architectural. In a sense, this is how it should be – stately homes are not imposing, impersonal edifices devoid of spirit and character. In many cases they represent the hearth, hall and kitchen of a family, with all the laughter, sadness and idiosyncrasies that family life can bring.

It follows that the greatest interest of all is shown in any sign which reads 'private', 'no public', or 'family only'. These present an irresistible challenge to an enterprising visitor. I remember one incident involving my mother when a group, who must have climbed over the ropes, ignoring several 'private' signs en route, strolled in as she was luxuriating in her bath one morning.

'I think you've come in the wrong way,' she said as imperiously as her situation would allow.

'Sorry,' they replied and shot off, leaving my mother to ponder the strange intrusion ...

This is just an instance of how public meets private. As often as not it is the owner and not the paying visitor who comes off worse. So please don't see condescension where it is not intended – read our stories in the right spirit and you will learn that, in the corridors and bed chambers of stately homes, as in all walks of life, humour is universal; and that few retain their dignity for very long.

A quick word about guides. All stately home owners would praise their guides, a unique and dedicated breed, who work anti-social hours and inconvenient days, giving up their bank holidays and Sunday lunches at a moment's notice. Why do they do it? Not for the money, that's for sure. If they are paid at all, and many aren't, it is usually little recompense for the travelling involved. No, they're motivated I think, by love – love for the house and its contents, and affection for the family associated with or actually living in it. If all this seems a little sentimental, then you should bear in mind that total devotion has its price. Most guides are convinced they know more about the house than anyone else, and rarely suffer fools gladly. Any visitor who has the temerity to question the accuracy of a guide's rhetoric quickly learns not to.

At the magnificent Chatsworth House in Derbyshire, home to the Duke of Devonshire, there is a chapel, in which is displayed a glass painting of 'The Wedding Feast at Canaan'. When, on one occasion, the guide mistakenly described it as a representation of 'The Last Supper', a voice from the back of the tour party piped up to say that it couldn't possibly be, as there were women in the painting. The guide reeled around on his heels to face the unbeliever, and remarked, 'No, sir, I think you'll find I'm right. This is the "Chatsworth" version of "The Last Supper".' Utterly false of course, but enough to stop the visitor in his tracks.

Many of the stories in the book, you will notice, are set at Weston Park. The reason for this is simple – I live next door. I do not mean to suggest that our seventeenth-century family seat has a monopoly on diverting aristocratic tales, but simply that because of my closeness to the house and its history I find it easier to go into detail, and can paint what I hope is a rounded, personal picture. It might be appropriate, therefore, to give a little background information into how Weston came to be. This is easiest done by a description of the founder, my ancestor Lady Wilbraham.

She was born Elizabeth Mytton, heiress of Weston and its estates, and married Sir Thomas Wilbraham from Cheshire. Plainly not satisfied with the appearance of the then Manor House, she built Weston Park instead, teaching herself from Palladio's *First Book of Architecture* which was first published in English in 1663. With the assistance of a foreman, Sam Grice, the house was completed in 1671.

Lady Wilbraham evidently developed a taste for designing her own properties, because in the years that followed she erected a stable block at Weston, demolished her husband's house at Woodhey and put up a replacement, knocked down a Norman church in the grounds and rebuilt that. It is not known how much her husband was consulted during this period; from the portraits of the couple that hang in the drawing room, which show a demonstrative, determined wife and a less than virile husband, it would seem very little.

Nowadays, though it is owned by a charitable foundation, Weston Park is run very much as a commercial business. The operating company, Weston Park Enterprises, ploughs the profits back into the continuing improvement and restoration of the house, its contents and gardens. When people ask me, as they occasionally do, why it is so successful, I always like to make the utterly facetious remark, 'Well, luckily, my ancestor

Lady Wilbraham had the foresight to build Weston between the M6 and the M54, with easy access to Birmingham city centre.' This may seem like asking for a punch in the face, but in many ways we are indeed fortunate to be so close to the motorways, and to Britain's second largest city – a propitious accident of history!

Whatever the faults of this book and its author, I sincerely hope that it will go some way to demystifying the shrouded figure of the stately-home owner, and showing that peers aren't always as stuffy and eccentric as they sometimes appear. Many misconceptions thrive, but perhaps one of the most hurtful is the charge that, when in the House of Lords, many of us appear to be taking a nap. Little speakers are set into the tops of the seats, so that when a member has his head turned halfway round, he is in fact listening intently to the debate, and not recuperating from a night on the brandy. Most of the time anyway ...

Mistaken Identities

Titles get most of the British totally confused, including many of those who are themselves titled. How, for instance, do you start a letter to a Duke? Do you begin 'Your Grace'? Do you begin 'Dear Duke'? Or is it 'My Lord Duke'? Answer: all of them are right under different circumstances! As a matter of fact when I consulted a fellow peer on the correct way to address the Duke of Devonshire, he told me, 'Start the letter "Dear Devonshire"! I always do! He'll undoubtedly start his "Dear Bradford"!'

Why are Marquesses 'The Most Honourable', when Earls and Viscounts are 'The Right Honourable'? Why is it that, with some Lords and Ladies, you put a 'The' in front, and with others you don't? Consult a higher oracle than me!

What is the natural connection between an Earl and a Countess, apart from the fact that they are man and wife? Surely the French handle the situation much better with their 'Comte et Comtesse'.

A Marquess sounds as if he should be a woman. He most definitely isn't! And how on earth does his wife get to be a Marchioness? As they themselves will tell you, their distinctive titles often cause plenty of confusion, and not a little amusement.

And why is a Baron only ever 'Lord', when a Viscount, an Earl or a Marquess is called 'Lord' in speech or at the start of a letter, but addressed by his title on an envelope? Bewildered? You should be!

Of course, there is also the geographical illogicality – why can't people with titles live where they ought to? The Duke of Devonshire shouldn't be in Derbyshire, while the Earl of Suffolk and Berkshire has a choice of two counties, and

13

chooses to reside in Wiltshire.

Our family is often charged with the same absurdity. Our home is nowhere near Bradford in Yorkshire, or even Bradford-upon-Avon. Our accusers are wrong, however. My ancestor, when he was made a Baron in 1794, actually took his title from 'The Hundred of South Bradford' which is in Shropshire, where we live to this day.

When the son of the first Baron was created both an Earl and a Viscount in 1815, he again used the name Bradford for the Earldom. For his Viscountship he chose the small delightful country town of Newport, Shropshire, which is also situated in 'The Hundred of South Bradford'. Therefore almost all dynastic assumptions about our family origins tend to be inaccurate, as 'our' Newport is usually thought to be the one in South Wales!

Unfortunately nobody has ever got round to explaining these facts to the council officials of Bradford, Yorkshire. With the result that Weston Park is perennially pursued by staff from the Education Department, anxious to organize school visits to see the family seat of their Earl. I gently put them right, of course, but try never to turn away potential business! Unfortunately, in embarrassment and confusion, they discover all sorts of reasons, usually the obvious one of distance, not to make an actual booking. The main mission in life of every retiring Lord Mayor of Bradford is, it would seem, to write a new history of the city, and naturally 'their' Earl is always invited to buy a copy.

The only other connection between Newport and Bradford that I am aware of is that a magnificent School of Van Dyck portrait of Mountjoy Blount, Earl of Newport – no relation whatsoever – hangs in the dining room at Weston Park.

Tragically he was killed at the Battle of Bradford, during the Civil War. He was leading his Army of Cavaliers far too enthusiastically in their attack on the City. Like all good commanders he lead from the front, but left a one-hundred-yard gap between himself and the rest of his troops, which was perhaps a little rash. He duly paid the price, as the defenders promptly dispatched him and then surrendered against the overwhelming odds; he was apparently the only casualty of that particular conflict!

The whole area of titles is a complete minefield for the socially aware or those who wish to be correct in their form of address. Except that you find that the only people who really don't mind what they are called are the recipients themselves. Like me, they tend to be simply bemused by the myriad ways that people or computers get muddled.

People have particular problems when it comes to addressing a letter or having to introduce you at a gathering. It is as if they have carefully practised what they are going to say for so long, that when it comes to the vital second, they suddenly forget everything and revert to the first thought that comes into their heads.

At a motorcycle rally at Weston Park, the bikers from the Vincent HRD Owners' Club, in their leather gear, lined up their magnificent machines on the front of the house. The organizer gathered them all around, and then, with earnest concentration, proceeded to introduce my wife and I as Countess Bradford and Count Bradford, making me sound rather like an American jazz pianist.

In 1965, at the tender age of seventeen, I went to Ghana on VSO (Voluntary Service Overseas) to teach at a secondary school on the northern border. This constituted my year off between leaving Harrow and going up to Trinity College, Cambridge.

It was an enormously rewarding experience, and in many ways taught me more about the world and personal responsibility than school or university ever did. But other aspects of that period were pretty bleak, particularly with regard to the food and its edibility. I lost a lot of weight, almost three stone, in ten months. Of course it didn't help that during that period I also caught malaria (three times), dysentery and even typhus fever.

I decided, therefore, during the Easter holidays, to travel to Lome in Togo, and experience some real French cooking, as well as do some sightseeing. At that time you needed to apply for a visa before you could leave, and it being Easter, offices kept opening and closing, making the whole process an extremely protracted one.

Eventually, after one week the visa was issued. To my horror the name on it was 'Mr Right H.', taking a lead from my passport, which read 'The Right Hon. The Viscount Newport', which I believe was incorrect anyway, as the title was only a 'courtesy' one.

I tried to explain that the name on the visa was wrong, and after a short wait a second visa was granted to 'Mr Right H.N.'; when the third one read 'Mr Right H.N. Viscount', I gave up and left on the trip, unofficially so to speak, whilst there was still some time before the summer term started.

Needless to say, there was no problem at the Togolese border, travelling in either direction! And the food was well worth the trip. I think I had heartburn for three days.

An American guide book, *Frommers '94*, gave a marvellous write-up to my restaurant, Porters, in Covent Garden, praising our range of traditional pies, real English puddings, and describing the 'friendly, informal and lively atmosphere in comfortable surroundings'; all that any restaurateur would wish for! Unfortunately the report lost some credibility in stating that 'This place is owned by the current Earl of Bedford, who is a frequent visitor'.

Particularly strange, though, are the ways that my wife and I have been addressed on envelopes. Frequently these result from the mistakes of computers, which seem ill-equipped to handle such a complicated concept as the British title system.

They merely mangle everything up, and eventually – presumably according to the way in which they are programmed – choose some very strange surnames. For example, 'Dear Mr Righthon', which is fair enough in some ways! But you do fail to understand the thinking behind 'Dear Mr Of', or once, 'Ms The Earl of Bradford'. Has someone been talking behind my frock? Funny that, because I don't usually wear one. Or maybe it was a feminist computer!

More common are the times when you get promoted to 'The Duke of Bradford' or demoted to the ranks of 'Mr E.O. Bradford', or 'Mr Earl'.

Thanks to the computer's habit of reducing an 'of' to an 'O', the Irish branch of the family often makes an appearance, in 'The Earl O Bradford'.

My absolute favourites are when, inexplicably, I get an 'l' deducted from my title, to become either 'The Ear of' or 'The 7th Ear of'. The first time this happened I pinned an envelope, addressed to 'The 7th Ear of Bradford' on the notice board at Weston, with a note which read, 'Watch out! Now I am listening to you with seven ears!' Shortly afterwards my wife was delighted to receive a letter written to 'The Earless of Bradford'. So despite appearances she has no hearing equipment, and I have rather too much!

The Countess Bra
Woodlands House
Weston Under Lizard
Shifnal
Salop
TF11 8PX

Lord Lichfield,
Earl of Bradford
Weston Park,
Weston-U-Lizard

EARL R T ORLANDO
WOODLANDS HOUSE
MILL LANE
WESTON UNDER LIZARD
SHIFNAL SHROPSHIRE
TF11

Earl Richard T O Bradford Of
Bridgeman
Richard T O Bridgeman
Bradford Estate Office
Weston-Under-Lizard
SHIFNAL TF11 8JU

EARL RICHARD T O BRADFORD OF BRIDGEMAN
Proprietor
Richard T O Bridgeman
Bradford Estate Office
Weston-Under-Lizard
Shifnal Shropshire
TF11 8JU

Ms The Earl Of Bradford
Woodlands House
Weston Under Lizard
Shifnal
TF11 8PX

MR RICHARD THOMAS ORLNDO BRIDGEMAN BRADFORD
THE BRADFORD ESTATE OFC
SHIFNAL SALOP,LONDON
UK

Dear Mr The

Rt On Earl of Bradford
Offoxney Farm
Tong
Shifnal
Shropshire
TF11 8QA

Earl of B - R Thomas
Woodlands House
Mill Lane Weston Under Lizard
Shifnal Shropshire
TF11 8PX

EAR BRADFORD
WOODLANDS HOUSE
WESTON UNDER LIZARD
SHIFNAL
SHROPSHIRE
TF11 8LE

OF BRADFORD ESQ.
WESTON PARK
SHIFNAL,
SHROPSHIRE

TF11 8NA

D J Weston Brad
Bradford Estates
Westonwig Izard
Shipnal
Salop TF11

The R Earl
Woodlands House
Of Bradford
Western Under Lizard
Shifnal Shropshire
TF11 8PX

Earl o Bradford
Weston Park
Shropshire

The Fleet Manager
The Righton The Seventh Earl
Woodlands House
Of Bradford
Western Under Lizard
Shifnal Shropshire
TF11 8PX

The Ear of Bradford
Weston Park
Nr Shifnal
Shropshire
TF11 8LE

Dear The Ea Bradford,

The Earless of Bradford
Weston Park
Nr Shifnal
Shropshire TF11 8PX

Earl of Newport
Weston Park.
Weston under Lizard
SHROPSHIRE

My wife and I went to stay in the South of France for our eighth wedding anniversary. One night we booked into a restaurant by the harbour at Beaulieu. When we arrived the manager, embarrassingly, denied any knowledge of us and tried to turn us away saying he was fully booked.

Looking around the tables, on which were propped little cards where the customer's name was inscribed, I discovered a reservation under 'Monsieur Earlov'. Recognizing this name to be my own – despite a misappropriated Russian flavour – I again queried the manager and we had our booking honoured.

A recent visit to Florida reconfirmed the fact that the Americans still have no idea about British titles. Even British Airways, though we had filled in all their forms properly, had me down as 'E Lord Bradford'.

I explained the situation to a receptionist at the Disney Beach Club and, after negotiating total incredulity on her part, managed to get us registered as 'The Earl of Bradford and family'. Unfortunately this ensured that no telephone calls or messages got through to me, as the computer had my surname down as 'Of Bradford'. All callers, despite their insistence to the contrary, were told that there was no 'Bradford' staying at the hotel.

The second hotel, the South Seas on Captiva Island, managed little better. I couldn't understand why, but when we entered the grounds and were given a blue card by the security guard to stick on our car windscreen, it had 'B. Bradford' scribbled on it. Everything became clearer at reception when we checked in. Surprise, surprise, I was down as 'Mr Bridgeman Bradford'!

Many years ago I went to stay at the Lobster Pot, a hotel in Mousehole, near Penzance, mainly to go shark fishing with Frankie and Phil Wallis, two brothers I had met on a previous trip, and who specialized in taking visitors shark and mackerel fishing.

On the third evening, I was introduced to Charlie Greenhaugh, a wonderfully charismatic, truly Cornish character, who kept the Swan Pub opposite; tragically he lost his life a few years later in the appalling lifeboat disaster.

Charlie was someone you felt privileged to have known, though at the time he just kept you so amused that you didn't tend to think about the other aspects of his very active life. In his strong local burr, he told me, 'It's funny meeting you, cos the night before last, Frankie Wallis was in the pub, and after about his third or fourth pint, I said, well Frankie how's things then? To which Frankie replied, "Well, I'm a bit worried, Charlie, I've got this 'ere bloody Lord comin' out with me tomorrow. I don't know what to call the bugger."

'Next night he was back in the pub, and after about his third or fourth pint, I asked him, how was that then Lord of yours today? He said, "Oh Charlie, that was all right, that was Richard. Known him for years. Never realized he had one of them funny titles." '

If titles represent a verbal minefield for the adults, for children they're an inscrutable mystery.

My grandfather passed away when I was nine years old. I remember that I wasn't allowed to go to the funeral, partly because it would disrupt my studies, but mainly because my school was in Kent, a considerable distance from Weston.

(It has always struck me as strange that I was sent quite so far away, when there were many other good schools much closer to home. My father for instance went to a place near Bromsgrove, which is just down the road. But as my sisters were also banished to a far corner of the country for their tuition and improvement, I had no cause to suspect my parents of reverse favouritism. An aversion to annoying little kids in general, well, possibly that was a different matter!)

The next time I saw a member of the family was when my father picked me up from Charing Cross station at the end of term. Before my grandfather died, I was referred to simply by my surname, Bridgeman, in the traditional manner of British preparatory schools, but since his death I'd been puzzling about what changes in nomenclature the sad event would bring. This, I believe, was only natural; I mean it's nice to know what your name is from time to time. But nobody had explained anything to me, and though I knew it must involve a fairly radical transformation, I couldn't for the life of me work out what that transformation might be. It took me half the journey home to summon up the courage and ask my father directly, 'Dad, what's my name now?'

'Richard,' he said, 'I have become the Earl of Bradford and you're the Viscount Newport.'

Whilst this answer was as simple and straightforward as it could be, it came as a bit of a bombshell, as you may imagine. It wasn't until my mother changed all the nametapes on my clothes, and the masters at school began calling me 'Newport' instead of 'Bridgeman', (which, if the truth be known, I'd been perfectly happy with) that I acclimatized to my new name.

My own children encountered similar difficulties when my father died: Alexander, my eldest, became Viscount Newport as I had done many years before. Harry, our second son, is known as the Hon. Harry Bridgeman.

So they started school as Newport and Bridgeman; two brothers with different surnames, if you like. At the end of their first day they came home and said to their mother, 'Mum, it's very strange, there's another pair of brothers in the school, and do you know, they've both got the same name!'

To Harry and Alexander, this seemed really rather odd.

About thirty years ago, my father paid a visit to Australia to look into the possibility of buying a farm out there. He travelled to a small town called Tiree, where he was met by the local bank manager, who'd been given the task of showing the Englishman around.

Unlike the British variety, the Australian bank manager is allowed to have a sense of humour, and my father's guide proved to be no exception. But he had no idea about English titles, and was too proud to ask. So he took the 'coward's way out' which is to slur any introduction by running the words of the title into each other as follows: 'Morning to you, Charlie! I'd like you to meet an English friend of mine. This is Erl Brfrd.'

The inhabitants of Tiree, understandably, chose to call my father 'Earl' as if it was his Christian name. They'd wave at him from their porches, shouting out as he passed by, 'Afternoon, Earl', or 'Good day to you, Earl!' A friendly bunch, and my father thought it best to leave them uncorrected in the circumstances.

However, the day after my father left, the bank manager got caught out by a report in the local newspaper telling how the Earl of Bradford, a prominent member of the British aristocracy, had been visiting Tiree to look for a farm. He then had to put up with an enormous number of aggrieved local citizens asking, 'Why didn't you tell us that nice bloke Earl was a Pommie Lord?' I'm not sure he ever lived it down!

We often find people wandering around Weston Park looking rather bewildered. It is generally my practice to go up to them, ask if I can be of help and try to steer them in the right direction.

One day I was looking out of the office window, and saw this smartly dressed young man, briefcase in hand, looking particularly lost and worried. I popped out and cheerily asked, 'Can I help you?'

'Yes please. I'm the local Kenco rep, and I've been looking all over the place for this pub I'm supposed to call in on – The Earl of Bradford.'

There was only one possible reply, 'You're talking to the pub; what can I do for you?'

Twenty years ago, when I was still The Viscount Newport, I owned a restaurant on the Kings Road in London called Paupers. (The name referred to the reasonable prices, rather than any intrinsic feature of the customers, in case you're wondering.) The restaurant was invariably full to overflowing, and on certain evenings clients who hadn't booked had to wait a good while for a seat.

One night I was managing the place, when a classic example of a recognized London phenomenon, the Hooray Henry (*Arrogantius Maximus*), came down the stairs – pinstriped suit, pinstriped shirt, pinstriped attitude ... I instantly identified him as a jumped-up young idiot out merely to impress, the sort of public school product that only finds employment in the army, or failing that an estate agency.

People say Hooray Henrys speak with a plum in their mouth; this one had several pomegranates and a summer fruit bowl in his: 'Eough,' he said superciliously. 'My good man, have you got a table for four?'

'No we haven't, I'm afraid,' I replied, 'because we are completely full. But I would be delighted to give you a table in about fifty minutes.'

'Eough, I seeee,' he whined, then came back with, 'Ectually I'm a friend of Lord Newport's, you know. Are you sure you haven't got a table?'

'Sir, as I said, we are full at the moment. I can only repeat my offer to give you a table in fifty minutes.'

'Eough,' he retorted, sounding more like a donkey by the minute, 'I'm not sure that's good enough! You wait till Viscount Newport hears about this! I'm going to tell him about you myself.' With that, he coughed indignantly and stalked off – to inform me of my own terrible behaviour, I expect.

At the entrance to my restaurant, Porters, in Covent Garden, there is a sign which reads, rather cryptically, 'Always one on when the others are off.' Below this is my name, followed by the names of the four restaurant managers. Against each is a little of piece of wood which slides across to expose either 'in' or 'out' – the idea being to personalize the dining experience for the customers.

One lunchtime I was standing by the board as two girls, who had just finished their meal, were preparing to pay; one of them pointed at my name and the 'in' word next to it, and said, 'I wouldn't believe that if I were you.'

The other girl asked, 'Why not?'

The first one stated, 'Well, him at the top, he's not here anyway, he's in America.'

'How could you know that?' the second queried.

'Nigel Dempster says so!' exclaimed the other in triumph.

Goodwood in Sussex – less of a stately home, more of an empire. Quite apart from the magnificent house, the grounds encompass a racecourse, an aerodrome, a motor testing circuit, a hotel and golf and country club.

When the 3rd Duke of Richmond died in 1806, he left debts to the amount of £5 million. This was partly due to the fact that he twice enlarged the Jacobean hunting lodge which was originally handed down to him, adding more and more princely rooms to house both his numerous guests and his ever growing art collection. And to this day Goodwood House is still full of guests and great works of art.

Stately piles can have a peculiar effect on the uninitiated. In the mid-60s, an American gentleman and his wife came to visit Goodwood on an open day. There was definitely something strange about this couple. According to a guide on duty that day, they kept asking if the 9th Duke was at home, and seemed oddly fearful of meeting him. When finally asked to explain their anxiety, the husband recounted the following tale.

The story began during the war when they owned an apartment in Washington. Next door had lived an English couple, Freddie and Betty Richmond, whom they got to know very well. So well, in fact, that when the Richmonds had to return to England, the neighbours accepted an invitation to go and stay with them at their home, Goodwood.

A few years later the Americans were able to take up the offer when they made their first trip to England. Freddie warmly renewed his invitation and arranged to meet them at the station where the reunion was emotional on both sides.

Things began to go wrong, however, as they neared the house. The guests had imagined for their old friends a cosy

'Dunrovin' semi. What they saw as they rounded the drive filled them with horror – the Richmonds lived in a palace! Not only that but there were scores of butlers too, who snatched away their luggage as soon as they entered the front porch. Terror mounting and unassuaged by tea in the library, they went up to their rooms only to find the bags had been unpacked and their clothes neatly hung up in cupboards. This was too much to cope with – they didn't explain exactly how they escaped but flee they did, minds a blur.

This was the end of the story. Now here they were, back at Goodwood ten years on, enjoying the glorious treasures they might have shared with their good friends, Freddie and Betty, once upon a time.

It is a mark of the 9th Duke's modesty, staff tell me, that he didn't dream that trappings could make any difference to a firm friendship.

Shortly after the war, The 9th Duke of Richmond and Gordon was invited out to Detroit to look at the motor business because of Goodwood's well-known close connections with classic racing cars.

Arriving at the hotel, the Duke had to wait at the reception desk for some time in order to check in. When he finally got to the head of the queue, and gave his name to the receptionist there, she was none too cooperative: 'No, I'm sorry, sir,' he was smilingly told. 'But we have no reservation under the name of Richmond. Perhaps you wouldn't mind going to the back of the queue. Have a nice day!'

Thirty minutes later, after another intensive queuing session, he was back again. The receptionist was as intransigent as before: 'No, I'm sorry, sir … Would you mind …?'

By this time the Duke had had enough of waiting in line,

and felt that his only chance of escape from a life spent queuing in a Detroit hotel lay in a confrontation with the manager.

'Look, young lady,' he growled at the receptionist, 'I will say it again – I am the Duke of Richmond and Gordon, I have a room booked here, tonight, and I want to see someone in charge.'

At last the manager was found. It was clear from his bumptious attitude that he hadn't the slightest idea the Englishman had suffered any kind of delay. He strode up, and shaking the bemused aristocrat energetically by the hand, boomed: 'Say, Duke Richmond, so nice to have you here. A real honour for our hotel. Welcome to Detroit, we have the most spectacular room for you, and another one for your friend Gordon, just across the corridor.'

Before the present Duke of Richmond and Gordon succeeded to the dukedom, his title was The Earl of March. On one occasion he was organizing a conference in Oxford, and had to supervise the delivery of a truckload of audio-visual equipment. When it arrived, he stopped the driver of the lorry to give him his instructions, 'Ah, would you drive in through that gate please, and unload the equipment through the door opposite.'

'Right, mate,' said the lorry driver, and then rather truculently, 'And who might you be, when you're about?'

Slightly taken aback at this unexpected show of belligerence, he could only think to say, 'Why, I'm The Earl of March.'

Like a flash, the lorry driver shot back, 'Well mate, in that case, I'm The Earl of Bleeding April!'

The Earl of Shrewsbury and Talbot is the Premier Earl of Great Britain. This makes him sound extremely important, but actually means that his title was the earliest existing Earldom granted. He can, therefore, 'Lord' it over more recent ones like my own or Patrick Lichfield's.

Before he succeeded to the title, he was known by the courtesy title of Lord Ingestre. One day he called in to a friend's business in Stoke-on-Trent to meet him and go out for lunch. On arrival he walked up to the receptionist and announced himself to her. She closed the glass screen separating her office from reception and picked up a phone. Owing to the narrowness of the partition, the Earl could hear quite easily as she called her boss.

'Excuse me, Mr Corn, but there's a Rep from Nor Industries who's here to see you. Will you be coming down to meet him, or shall I say you're out?'

Some years ago the Earl of Plymouth was staying at his flat in London when a large parcel covered in exotic Far Eastern stamps turned up on his front door. In eagerness and excitement he and his wife opened the package only to find a tatty kitbag containing various personal objects and a small urn full to the brim with ashes.

The Earl was puzzled. He knew for a fact that none of his relations had either moved to Singapore or expired in the last few weeks. The idea that one of them had gone and done both, without letting him know, was impossible to credit. But the address was most clear – Earl of Plymouth, England.

Several days of detective work later, the mystery was finally unravelled. It seemed a certain merchant seaman had died three weeks earlier whilst working in the Far East. The body had been cremated out there, and the captain of his ship had sent the remains to the only firm of funeral directors he knew, a company by the name of 'Earl' based in Plymouth.

In a solicitor's letter the peer proposed that the directors might like to insert a comma into their trading name, which, rendering it 'Earl, of Plymouth', might prevent a repeat of this morbid mix-up.

The *real* Earl of Plymouth states, 'I am glad to say that no more commodities for this business have arrived at any of my residences.'

From Lord Shuttleworth

The wording on peers' passports frequently causes confusion abroad. Mine reads 'The Right Honourable The Lord Shuttleworth'.

Once, arriving at a very hot and overcrowded Delhi airport, it took me three hours from joining the Immigration/Passport queue to reach the desk. It became apparent that a computer was chiefly to blame for the delay.

In an effort to assist, I suggested that the word 'Shuttleworth' be keyed in first. The screen promptly flashed up NOT CLEARED FOR ENTRY, and the operator looked at me as if I was mad. Clearly unimpressed with my advice, she deleted 'Shuttleworth' and inserted just 'The Lord' – which in turn was NOT CLEARED FOR ENTRY.

A number of other variations on my name were tried during a frustrating few minutes, until at last the computer recognized my booking under the single word 'Honourable'. This it most graciously CLEARED FOR ENTRY, and with a smile and a greeting, 'Welcome, Mr Honourable', I was admitted to India.

The Marquess and Marchioness of Tavistock, owners of Woburn Abbey, were spending some time in New York. During their visit Lady Tavistock went shopping at Bloomingdale's, one of the world's most famous department stores.

When she was at the counter paying for her purchases, she gave the sales lady her name. The latter looked a little perplexed and asked, 'Tell me, if you're a "Martianess" is your husband a "Martian"?'

The Viscount Massereene and Ferrard was much amused on one occasion to be addressed as 'The Viscount Maserati and Ferrari'. As he said at the time, 'If only it were true!'

When the late Marquess of Exeter was heavily involved with the Olympic Games, he received many wonderfully addressed letters, especially from Africa. The family's favourite was one sent to 'Lord Et Cetera'.

Viscount Norwich remembers a hotel receptionist in Ljubljana, who, baffled by the name on his passport, The Right Honourable John Julius Cooper, the Viscount Norwich, logged him in simply as Mr Right. 'What I have always wanted to be in fact,' he says.

On another occasion he was addressed, rather sinisterly, as 'The Vice Count Norwich', and once, more disarmingly, as 'The Discount Norwich', 'which gave considerable pleasure to my friends and family'.

In 1992, Sir Reresby Sitwell, Bt, owner of Renishaw Hall in Derbyshire, received a four-page letter from a company trying to sell 'Sister Gitwell' a timeshare. Soon after, he wrote back to the firm, '... I have never heard of this surname although I do realize it bears a strong resemblance to my own. Regrettably neither my wife nor I have nursing abilities, and in view of the new story of the bogus American doctor perhaps it is just as well. All the same, I must admit to fancying the name of "Sister Gitwell" for myself.'

The present Earl of Rosebery, when Lord Primrose, filled in a library application form with just his surname, the Mr/Mrs crossed out and 'Lord' inserted. The form was processed and a membership card eventually issued to a 'Miss Primrose Lord'. It lasted him many years!

Lord Aberdare enjoyed the manipulations of one computer's brain. It transformed him, tersely, into 'The Rt. Ho. Ab.'.

The Marquess of Hertford writes: 'I was flying back from the army in Egypt. But I missed the aeroplane on which I had been booked because it never occurred to me to look in the alphabetical list of passengers under M rather than H. A few years later, I booked a flight from London to Copenhagen – again I failed to find my name on the passenger list, but was eventually allowed to travel as "Mr Marcus".'

L ord Romsey tells me that his mother, The Countess Mountbatten of Burma, regularly receives mail addressed to 'The Burma'. This makes her sound rather like a battleship, which couldn't be further from the truth!

C omputers have the greatest difficulty with titles. The processing of credit and debit cards presents the machine with a major problem – usually one of space. Programmed to accept no more than 18 characters, a name like 'the Marchioness of Tavistock' is enough to send even the most sophisticated software into electronic convulsions.

You will have seen, perhaps, how I have been addressed over the years.

The owners of Woburn Abbey, Lord and Lady Tavistock have also had their fair share of misconstructions. On cards, Marquess of Tavistock is generally either 'M O Tavistock', 'Marquess Of Tavist', or simply 'Marquess Tavistock'. Notice the way the 'of' has been endowed (wrongly) with a capital O, as if it were a middle name. Often the word 'of' is rendered just 'O', as in 'Earl O Bradford'.

This is because computers like middle names to be abbreviated to a capital, if possible. They evidently cannot comprehend the improbability of someone actually being christened 'Of'.

But computer operators are fiercely protective of their contraptions. Although some are willing to enter the name manually, others look at you stony faced, and contest that you have a right to a title. If the computer doesn't accept it, they say, then the title can't be real – you must have made it up. More radical are the occasions when the computer refuses to acknowledge that you exist at all.

When Mid Bedfordshire District Council computerized the Community Charge information form, despite written confirmation from the parties involved that Lord Tavistock was the Marquess of Tavistock (forenames: Henry Robin Ian) and Lady Tavistock, the Marchioness of Tavistock (forenames: Henrietta Joan), they both became very simply 'Tavistock', Woburn Abbey. Shortly after, this was changed to 'M O Tavistock', Woburn Abbey. One of them had disappeared!

Naturally only one Community Charge demand was issued, in the name of 'M O Tavistock'.

Only when the Community Charge became the Council Tax, and M O Tavistock, in an act of breathtaking honesty, refused to apply for a single person household discount did the District Council at last agree to look into the matter.

Berkeley Castle in Gloucestershire is one of Britain's most historic stately homes. Not many can boast of having been celebrated by Shakespeare; nor of having been held in the possession of the same family for over 800 years; nor of having had a King (Edward II in 1327) murdered within its walls. Such is the story of Berkeley – a Norman fortress begun in 1177, and still lived in as a family home.

A story told by Eiler Hansen, custodian of the castle, concerns a question of protocol. An anonymous Lady had invited many titled guests, including a Duke and Duchess, to a grand charity dinner. She had also asked the Aga Khan, but secretly expected him to turn down the invitation.

However, when he accepted, Her Ladyship realized she had a dining dilemma on her hands. Where at the top table do you sit the Aga Khan? She consulted *Debrett's Peerage*, where she found this pearl of wisdom: 'By his millions of followers the Aga Khan is regarded as a direct descendant of God. An English Duke takes precedence.'

Whether this tale (which is more than likely apocryphal) exposes the pretensions of *Debrett's* or the snobberies of the aristocracy I cannot say. Eiler informs me that in Denmark they use it more generally as a humorous stab at the British way of life. If that is true, we may have a few more years to wait before European cultural unity is achieved.

Eiler Hansen tells another story.

My name is Eiler Hansen and I happen to speak seven languages. One Sunday in September last year, the car park at Berkeley suddenly and unexpectedly became chock-a-block, and the ticket office telephoned me and asked if I would come and help out.

On arrival, I noticed that a small queue of cars had formed, the first vehicle being occupied by an irate German. I spoke to him in German, and politely asked him to be a little more patient.

Then another car pulled out in front of me, this one driven by a Dutchman who wanted to know the best route to Bath. I gave him instructions – in his native tongue. The German began honking his horn at the Dutchman who was blocking his path, so I shouted to the German to wait a minute.

Simultaneously a group of Swedish students, whom I'd met earlier in the day when I gave them an introduction to the castle – in Swedish – appeared at my side and tried to engage me in conversation. So I gently suggested to them that I was quite busy, and could they hang on for a few minutes.

At this point, the Dutchman, who had watched my performance, wound down his window again and said to me: 'You speak Nederlands to me, German to the fellow over there, and a language I do not know to those young people.

That is very rare in England. So why do you work as a car park attendant?'

There are many stories accumulated over the years about visitors who didn't realize they were talking to my father. Usually they'd come into the house and remark to the head guide, 'I must say, your gardener was enormously helpful and most informative about Weston Park.'

This was because my father loved pruning. He could often be seen wandering around the trees and shrubs, dressed not in a crown and coronet, but in clothes more appropriate to the work. The public naturally assumed that they'd met a particularly well spoken hedge-cutter – which in a sense they had.

Naworth Castle in Cumbria, a historic border fortress built in 1335, is now home to the Earl and Countess of Carlisle. The present Earl of Carlisle's great-grandfather went one better than my father. He actually got paid for being who he wasn't!

A committed and talented artist, he used to work in a large stone building which had once been a fuel house. One day a wagonette pitched up, unusually, right outside his studio. A group of visitors disembarked, anxious to view the castle.

The artist appeared from his studio, looking rather dishevelled in his stained cotton smock and dusty sandals. One of the party greeted him asking, 'Are you the painter?'

'I suppose I must be,' answered the owner, a little taken aback.

'Would you hold our horses whilst we look round the castle?' the man casually inquired.

Feeling especially generous to the world that day, the proprietor agreed, and the party ambled off leaving him holding the reins. But after about an hour, he grew tired of his custodial responsibilities. Tying the animals to a rail, he went back inside to continue his painting.

When the visitors at last returned from their tour, the artist popped out of his lair just in time to be thanked by the whole party. They tipped him a gold sovereign for his labours which, the family say, was the only money he ever earned for doing a job in his life.

Conversation between the 10th Duke of Richmond and a Heathrow check-in clerk

'I have a booking, my name is Richmond.' (Whirring of computer.)

'I'm sorry but we have no booking for you.'

'I think you have – here is my card.' (Frantic whirring of computer.)

'Ah yes, Mr Duck, is it?'

'Yesss …' (Long sigh.)

Conversation the next day in Brussels

'Hello, my name is Richmond, I have a booking.' (Computer noises.)

'I'm sorry but we have no booking under that name.'

'I see, well here is my card.' (Lots of computer noises.)

'Oh – are you Mr The?'

'Yesss …' (Total resignation.)

The 11th Duke of Northumberland who owns, among others, two magnificent buildings – Syon House, set in its own park in Brentford, Middlesex, and Alnwick Castle in Northumberland – explains how often it is the confusions arising from the house's name that provoke the most bizarre results.

One member of staff was verbally harassed at some length over the telephone by an irascible gentleman demanding that she send him a certificate for his company. The employee couldn't really understand what on earth he wanted, nor indeed why he wanted it, so she asked him to write a letter outlining his request.

The letter came through some days later, addressed to 'Psion Park'. It turned out that the man wanted a license authorizing him to sell Psion Computers.

And … some people choose Syon as a venue for the strangest reasons. 'Sony', for instance, held a launch there on the basis that Syon is an anagram of Sony.

A maintenance man for the Albury Estate forestry department once came across a rusty old Mini parked in the yard at Syon House. He looked at it for a while, taking in the crumbling wheel arches and the huge dents on the bonnet, and was just about to take action when the Duke of Northumberland appeared at his side.

'Blimey, Your Grace,' fumed the employee, 'somebody must have dumped this load of old junk here last night. I'll ring the scrap man and have it taken away immediately.'

'Actually,' said the Duke, 'the car is mine, and I'm going to use it in London. It should stop me being recognized so often.'

Two men from the Northumberland estate were dispatched to London one day to deliver some oil paintings for restoration. Reaching the metropolis, they couldn't find anywhere to park, so they drove into St James's Palace, and plonked the vehicle in a space clearly reserved for 'Heads of State Only'.

'If anyone asks,' said the older man to the younger, hopping out of the car, 'tell 'em you're on official business for the Duke of Northumberland. That should do the trick.' He then grabbed the pictures from the boot and sped off in the direction of the restorers.

Returning half an hour later, he was ambushed by two stout policemen, who had carefully hidden themselves behind the rear end of the van. 'Are you the owner of this vehicle, sir?' asked one constable.

'Well, sort of ...' he mumbled, fearing imminent incarceration.

'In that case, Your Grace, would you mind waiting for five minutes whilst they finish changing the guard? Very sorry to bother you, sir.' Whereupon the policeman saluted, and stiffly marched away.

The employee, at once astonished and relieved, ducked back into the car and heartily thanked the powers that be.

The Duke of Northumberland tells of a story from Washington, USA, involving Lord Montagu of Beaulieu, who was trying to call a friend on the telephone through a receptionist. The conversation is said to have started as follows: 'Hello, this is Lord Montagu. Could you put me through to — —, please?'

'Certainly, sir. Umm, could I ask ... is that "Lord" as in "Jesus"?'

The final word on computers should, I feel, be left to Lord Hailsham:

House of Lords

Dear Lord Bradford:

Thank you for yr: letter of 6 June.

Doubtless thousands of risible things have occurred to me in the course of my mis-spent life. But I have a memory like a sieve and there is only one which comes to mind here and now. If illustrates the vagaries of the computer in our present age.

The other day an envelope containing junk mail arrived at my home addressed

Quaintly to "Mr Of". It took me some
time to understand that my title is too
long for a computer to digest, and so
it took the "Of" out of "Hailsham of
St Marylebone". Intelligent things,
Computers. I wish I had kept the
envelope

        yrs · sincerely :

    Hailsham of St Marylebone
       a·k·a· "Mr Of"

The Doings of
M'Lords

Running a stately home requires you to be tough, resilient and impervious to wounding criticism. Where do proprietors receive their training for such a dangerous career, you may ask. Are there occupational degrees in the subject? Or is there a National Institute for the Rehabilitation of Owners? No.

But there has always been the English preparatory school. This is generally sufficient training for the prospective candidate. Once you've been towel-whipped in the showers, forced to copy out Psalm 23 and the entire Latin irregular verb system a thousand times, and subjected to the daily battery of the headmistress's piano-playing in morning assembly, then life in the real world comes as a pleasant surprise.

The nature of crime and punishment in these traditional establishments means that for those who survive, no ordeal is so great that it cannot be endured. Divorce, staff mutinies, Capital Gains Tax? Piddling, compared to an evening spent studying the cracks in the wall outside the headmaster's office. Bankruptcy, eviction, personal ruin? Trifling; the memory of eight hours' 'stone-picking' on a windswept crag in the Derbyshire Dales will soon put that into perspective.

Judging from recent experience with our children, modern prep schools have become more liberal. If that is the case then I fear for the future of privately owned historic houses. If the Battle of Waterloo was won on the playing fields of Eton, then the survival of Britain's stately homes will surely depend on regular flash-backs to cold showers at six o'clock in the morning.

Ex-alumni look back on their school days with a mixture

of longing and deep respect. Sir Reresby Sitwell was kind enough to send me a copy of the questionnaire sent to him by a research student. In it he was asked to answer a number of questions about his prep school. I include the questionnaire for historical reasons, as well as the insight it may give into the formation of that tenacious determinism innate to any owner.

Q.1. Why did your parents choose this school?
A. Probably because they recognized a fellow sadist in the headmaster.
Q.2. What things do you remember most about the school?
A. The bullying, the beatings, the bad food, the foul lavatories and the compulsory games.
Q.3. What aspects of the school did you particularly enjoy?
A. The day I left for good.
Q.4. Were there aspects of the school you did not enjoy?
A. Virtually every aspect.
Q.5. Overall, did you enjoy your time at the school? (Cross next to the one that applies.)
A. Very much   Mostly   Sometimes   Never XXX
Q.6. How would you describe the ethos of the school?
A. Grim.
Q.6. Did you enjoy games?
A. No.
Q.7. Would you agree with the claim that there was a 'games cult'?
A. Yes.
Q.8. Please write what you remember about particular members of staff.
A. I remember most of the staff – after fifty-three years – but, being a busy man, I cannot spare the time to record my memories of their individual eccentricities, cruelties and peccadilloes.
Q.9. Did any of the above have a special influence on you?
A. No, none of them.

Q.10. Looking back, do you think it was a worthwhile experience?
A. No.
Q.11. Do you wish to remain in contact with the school?
A. No.

It will come as no surprise that Sir Reresby is not a frequent visitor to his alma mater, nor does he participate in the annual Old Boys' football match. In fact, he has renounced for good any activity involving tight shorts, mud and a leather ball.

But Sir Reresby would be the first to admit that preparatory school gave him the wherewithal to withstand the sternest adversity. And for this, if nothing else, he is thankful to the unstinting savagery of teachers and staff at his pre-war prep school.

The 11th Duke of Northumberland reminisces about his father

During his Eton days my father came across such infamous masters as 'Bloody Bill' and 'Slippery Jesus'. He was desperately anxious not to be taught by them, but occasionally fate decided that he should be. It was with one of these that 'the pen' incident took place.

My father dropped his pen during class and the master said to him, 'Pick up your silver pen, Percy, and get on with your work.'

He retrieved the pen as instructed, but muttered under his breath, 'It's not silver, sir, it's gold.' The master heard him and replied dryly, 'Hmm, I see ... none of the lesser metals for Percy.'

This lovely touch of humour doubtless went over the

pupil's head, who was only a very young man at the time.

My father always used to say that though he himself got on well with 'Bobo', the late Duke of Roxburgh, he was not a very personable man.

He once found Bobo in a rare mood of reflection, pontificating on the subject of friendship. The Duke was saying: 'Oh, how fed up I am with these so-called Penny Steamers who go from peer to peer, exploiting my friendship, only so that they can indulge in my grouse moors, my sport and my wealth. What sort of people are these?'

My father could not resist the honest, though rather undiplomatic, answer, 'Well, Bobo, if it wasn't for such people you wouldn't have any friends at all.'

A final story of my father's. He had six aunts who were all brought up in the Catholic Apostolic Church. Their mother was a Drummond. She had stuck very close to the Faith ever since Sir Henry Drummond and Sir Edward Irving formed this strange sect at Albury in the early 1800s. Membership meant that you had to behave as if every day was your last on earth. In this way Catholic Apostolics, and only they, would be saved.

The sisters were encouraged to devote themselves to good works and religious readings. Any form of frivolity was frowned on by their puritanical mother. This deprivation obviously had a peculiar effect on their personalities.

When a visiting American professor was asked for his opinion on the Percy sisters he remarked, 'They are all charming females, except for Lady Mary, who is a woman.'

As it transpired, she was the only one who ever did succumb to holy matrimony; she became the mother of Gavin Maxwell.

The late Viscount Cobham was one of my father's greatest and closest friends. He was also one of the most naturally amusing characters I have ever met, and I was lucky and privileged to have him as one of my godfathers.

He and my father were contemporaries at Trinity College, Cambridge. They both got Firsts in 'Recreational Studies', an optional degree awarded to themselves by themselves after three years of conscientious self-indulgence. Sadly, this left little time for anything else, and on many occasions they were forced to abstain from more traditional scholastic pursuits.

The College rules were extremely strict in those days. You were only allowed out three nights a term, and had to be back in your rooms by midnight when the gates were locked. Naturally, this draconian system tended to conflict with the extra-curricular activities of many of the students. Those, like my father and his best friend, who were doing an unofficial course in 'Carousal Science', showed great ingenuity in devising practical solutions to the problem.

Charles Cobham, at that time The Hon. Charles Lyttelton, was in a rather fortunate position, as he was living in digs at Number 26, Trinity Street. This building adjoined the Great Gate of Trinity College. It had a separate entrance, which was locked at the same time as the rest of the college.

After considerable research, Charles hit upon a formula of sheer brilliance: a scheme which allowed him easy and undetectable access to his rooms after the closing-up time of twelve o'clock. (In actual fact, the route was not exactly original – generations of Trinity men had used it to mischievous effect – but this didn't dampen Charles's pioneering spirit in the slightest.) He found it was possible to climb on to the outside wall, clamber along its edge, then squeeze in through the bars of a toilet window which was conveniently situated on the first floor.

Like many a budding genius though, Charles was yet to

learn that theory does not always equate with practice. On his inaugural run he discovered to his horror that he was rather too well proportioned to fit through the bars of the window. He overcame this conundrum by removing all his clothes, which he then pushed between the bars. This allowed him to slide through the gap, Houdini-style, despite the likely onset of hypothermia.

On the second attempt, he uncovered another logistical flaw in the plan. Heaving himself on to the narrow ridge of the wall, he was surprised to be spotlit by a harsh light. Blinking furiously, he tried to ascertain the source, and quickly understood that he was in direct view of the college porter's window, which cast a strong beam outwards. He could see the porter clearly, grooming his hair with a large metal comb, which appeared to occupy his full attention, and Charles was able to lie flat against the top of the wall where he found the strength of the beam to be much weaker. If he lay prone for a while, and provided the porter didn't count astrology among his private hobbies, he would escape detection. After a few seconds, the light went out, and Charles could soon hear the porter's footsteps beneath him. The college servant was evidently doing his final patrol of the night, before he went to bed. This he duly did, and Charles was able to crawl along the wall, through the bars and into the confines of his rooms.

After the first two attempts, Charles became more confident and better practised in his nocturnal movements. He found that the porter kept to a precise timetable. If his light was on, this meant ten minutes' coiffuring at the most, followed by a five-minute inspection of the college grounds. As often as not, the porter was already asleep by the time Charles crept home.

A whole term went by in which Charles successfully used this way in and out of his college. But one cold February night his luck ran out. Assailing the wall in the usual way, and inching towards the toilet window, he removed all his clothes and slotted them through the space in the bars. He found this process more difficult than usual, for the night air was freezing and his fingers had practically seized up. He struggled manfully with his cuff-links, then his braces, as the Cambridge east wind sped from the Ural mountains over flat ground to the gates of Trinity College, where it cruelly lashed the nether regions of our intrepid hero. At length Charles reached a satisfactory state of nudity, and was just about to pull himself through the bars when he heard the unmistakable creak of the college main door. He peered through the gloom, espying the redoubtable figure of the porter who seemed to be looking in his direction. Charles hit the deck. 'This is most unusual,' he thought. 'What is the porter doing up at two o'clock in the morning? He should be in bed dreaming of the college nurse by now.'

Charles lay still, shivering in the arctic conditions. The sound of approaching footsteps grew louder as the student prowler pulled his underpants around his ears in a desperate attempt to conserve body heat. The porter was now directly beneath him, whistling contentedly in the manner of one who knows his time of glory has come. But he did not speak … he just stood there stamping his feet, permitting himself the occasional demonic chuckle.

Half an hour elapsed. Charles noted with alarm that his left leg had turned blue, and that icicles were beginning to form around the upper rim of his underpants. Still the porter lingered in silence. The naked aristocrat was on the point of conceding defeat, when he heard the porter retreating back to the warmth of the college. The heavy bolts of the main door slammed shut, and Charles prised himself from his lying position. As fast as his deep-frozen limbs would allow, he dragged himself through the bars and defrosted himself in front of his fire for two hours.

The following morning, as he went into college through

Great Gate for breakfast, the porter walked up to him, and knowingly remarked, 'Rather cold for the time of year, isn't it, sir?'

The first member of my family to rise to a prominent position was Sir Orlando Bridgeman, who was created a Baronet in 1660. He was an eminent lawyer and presided at the trial of the regicides of Charles I, condemning most of them to death. There are two pictures of him at Weston Park. In both he is wearing official robes, and with his dark hair and beard, allied to a seriously gloomy expression, he must have looked pretty terrifying to anyone standing in the dock.

He was created Lord Keeper of the Great Seal of England in 1667, and the large solid silver seal, which came in its own intricately woven bag, was duly entrusted to him. Unfortunately, he only held the post for five years; the King didn't care for his lack of cooperation in certain areas. Orlando refused, for instance, to grant pensions to the royal mistresses. Such an honest, upstanding individual could hardly condone this wanton squandering of the nation's resources, and he got the sack for it.

The experience of being fired must have altered his moral stance. Or maybe he just became very forgetful, because instead of handing back the Great Seal, as he ought, he had it melted down and – perhaps in an ironic reference to his former employer – remoulded into a Loving Cup.

In time, it was noticed at Court that the Seal had not been returned. A letter was swiftly dispatched, addressed to: 'Our right trusty and well-beloved Councillor Sir Orlando Bridgeman, Knight & Baronet, Keeper of the Great Seal of England.' The missive ran, 'Charles R. Our will and pleasure is that you forthwith deliver our Great Seal of England now in your custody.'

Inconveniently for the King, Sir Orlando died shortly after receiving this demand. However, it would seem that he never had the slightest intention of returning the state property. He had already bequeathed to his eldest son John 'that great piece of plate which was made of the Great Seal which I had in my custody'. It resides at Weston to this day, occasionally displayed as a centre piece on the main dining room table.

I should add, as a postscript, that the family no longer prides itself on an ability to misappropriate treasures of state. That particular talent died out with the first Baronet, although there have been times since when I wish it hadn't.

There is an old adage which states 'Never drink port after champagne.' It is most often quoted by those who have fallen foul of the liquid merger's immediate effects – loss of reason, loss of balance, loss of sexual morality – and its latent ones – apocalyptic hangover, acute paranoia, a stretch in prison.

One brave who played with fire, but lived to tell the tale was the great-grandfather of the present Viscount Massereene and Ferrard. Many years ago, he was enjoying a pleasant evening playing billiards and chatting to fellow members at his London club. After a particularly successful winning streak on the baize, he decided by way of celebration to open a few bottles of champagne.

Such moments are of course critical in the shaping of an evening, and before long he was, shall we say, oblivious to counsel. Brushing aside protestations from friends and barmen alike, he ventured to sample a bottle of vintage port.

An hour or so later, he found himself lurching erratically down St James's. A vigilant constable spotted him weaving between the street lamps and inquired in the courteous, gently disapproving tones the Mayfair police reserve for the (visibly drunk) upper classes: 'Good evening, sir. Can you tell me your name?'

Standing briskly to attention, the inebriated peer replied: 'Massereene and Ferrard. Both drunk.'

This winning repose was enough to throw the poor bobby. Mouth open wide, he made no effort to detain the Lord further, who resumed his uneven course through the streets of SW1.

The borders between fact and fiction are frequently merged in stories of the aristocracy. I would like to think that the following is wholly apocryphal. I doubt that it is ...

Many years ago a certain Lady had occasion to fire a pretty parlour maid. The girl stood silently as she received her dismissal, but finally spoke up: 'Your ladyship, now that I am sacked I feel able to speak my mind. I want to tell you that your husband, his Lordship, has often told me that I am a better housekeeper than you are, and a much better cook. So stick that in your pipe and smoke it! And what's more,' she added, 'I'm better in bed than you are!'

'Heavens!' said her Ladyship. 'Did my husband really say that?'

'No', replied the maid. 'The chauffeur said that.'

Wolseley Hall in Staffordshire, demolished in 1967, was formerly the ancestral seat of Sir Charles Wolseley, who is happy to relate some family history

The 7th Baronet, my namesake Sir Charles, embarked on a 'grand tour' of the Continent in 1789, having completed his formal education. His arrival in France coincided with the beginnings of the French Revolution. He found the ideas of the revolutionaries very appealing, and in fact took part in the subsequent storming of the Bastille.

Upon his return to England, he became a leader of the Radical Movement, which secured his arrest – for 'inciting crowds to riot in Stockport' – a fine of £1,000, and eventually his imprisonment. He was told that if he made a public apology, he would be released forthwith. Refusing to do anything of the kind, he opted for eighteen months in Abingdon Gaol instead, and actually professed to 'like it' there. Maybe this was because he was thoroughly immersed in the business of modernizing Wolseley Hall from his prison cell. The scheme was not entirely successful – he managed to transform a medieval gem into a gothic monstrosity, but little else.

It is also interesting to note that his youngest son was born two weeks before his release.

And some more recent, personal history

Aged nineteen, I was invited by an old school friend to stay at his parents' fine Georgian mansion near Kildalkey in Co. Meath. Arriving late in the afternoon I was asked to get ready for a family dinner to be followed by a drinks party.

After dinner, and the finishing of the port, loud bells heralded the arrival of the other guests, and the host led us back into the drawing room. Introductions and more alcohol … at about 11 p.m., owing in part to the copious quantity of liquid I had imbibed over the last several hours, I felt the need to relieve myself – but unable to see any of my hosts amidst the crowd, I had to prospect for the necessary alone, and without the faintest idea where I would find it.

At least eight doors opened off the lovely oval hall, and none of these seemed to offer much hope. The need by now being most pressing, I went out through the readily identifiable front door. Occasionally guests were still arriving, and the odd one leaving. I thought it best to follow a departee at a discreet distance down the front steps, into the night, and back towards the house. Outside it was pitch black, and very cold; unbuttoning myself as I approached a friendly looking wall, and in eager anticipation of blessed relief, I suddenly lost consciousness ...

Some time later – I've no idea how much – I came to my senses. I was lying, face upwards, on something soft and damp but couldn't for the life of me remember where I was or why I was there. One possible theory presented itself – I had passed out from too much wine, been carted upstairs and had, oh please no, wet the bed. It wasn't beyond the realms of probability ... but it was thankfully not the case. I realized that far from being tucked up in sodden sheets, I was in fact outside and, crucially, still bursting for a pee.

Getting to my feet unsteadily, I got that out of the way, and began exploring my environs. These were pretty restricted ... a tight passage, four feet wide at the most, with high vertical walls, and mossy earth underfoot. I looked up, and could see a narrow band of stars. Feeling like the sardine in the proverbial tin, I edged along the walls, searching for a way out. A hundred feet of clammy stone later I came to a dead end. So I retraced my steps.

In the meantime, it occurred to me that I had not after all been transported miraculously into another time dimension (my challenge: to slay the five-headed beast at the end of the tunnel) but had perhaps fallen down the house light-well which gives illumination to the basement and cellars.

This thought was of some comfort as I rounded several corners, and in time I met another obstruction – a coal shute blocking my path, but more importantly a means of escape!

I clambered on and up, only to find myself plunging downwards, scrabbling to get a purchase but failing dismally on the smooth, dust-covered surface. I landed in an undignified heap on a large pile of coke, and in total darkness. At length, having fallen over and into the coke several times, I located terra firma.

There are times when being a smoker has its natural advantages. One of these is that wherever you are, you always have some kind of lighting device to hand. Remembering mine, I took it out and, from its feeble glow, ascertained that I had fallen into some kind of boiler room, at the end of which was an open doorway. With repeated flicks of the lighter, I made my way towards it, went through, then into another room, and through another doorway. Finally, I espied a strip of light above me, and crawled up some steps to an ominous looking door. Behind this could be heard the faint sound of voices and clinking glasses.

Feeling sure that the door would be locked, and pondering how I would make my plight known in the noisy, later stages of an Irish drinks party, I shouldered against the wood, and came bursting out into the comparative glare of the oval hall again – exactly where my odyssey had begun.

My suit was a dark one, and didn't look too bad. So I shook myself down, wiped the dust from my hands, smoothed my hair, and returned to the fray in the drawing room, feigning an air of decorous nonchalance.

The soirée was still in full swing. But I couldn't help observing that those nearest were looking at me in a very strange manner. Gradually a wave of silence spread from them and over the whole assembly. A friend of mine broke the deadlock, and ushered me out of the room towards a mirror, which in my disturbed state, I had failed to notice. Peering at it, I realized why my appearance had brought the party conversation to an abrupt halt – my face was completely black, and streaked with blood.

Of course, I was asked to explain my condition, and the tale of the tunnel was told in full. One of my companions was outspokenly scathing and accused me of being *paralytically* drunk, whereas I perceived myself to be *merely* drunk. There is a difference. I challenged him to come and have a look, which he did, and I pointed him in the direction of the wall.

Moving forwards he fell straight down the light-well. I considered this evidence enough, and went back inside to rejoin the party.

Chavenage, near Tetbury in Gloucestershire is owned by David Lowsley-Williams, who has the rare distinction of being both proprietor and head guide. Normally, the tours are conducted by him personally. The striking Elizabethan house of mellow Cotswold stone, with its Cromwellian associations, has been used as a location for TV and film productions, including many episodes of the sequel to *Are You Being Served?*, now called *Grace and Favour*, and, more unusually, for *Noel Edmonds' House Party*. Agatha Christie's Poirot story, 'The Mystery at Styles Manor' was also filmed there.

But the real history lies in its regicidal roots. Colonel Nathaniel Stephens, MP, once owner of Chavenage was pressed to support Cromwell's intended measures against the life of King Charles I, despite the arguments of his conscience and those of his daughter. In a heated exchange she is said to have urged him to withhold his voice, and in a moment of particular enthusiasm, prophesied the extinction of his line if he became implicated in the murder of the monarch.

The May following, and with the King dispatched, Nathaniel was seized by a fatal illness. On his death-bed he called together all his relations in order to say his last goodbyes, and to express his deep regret at having participated in the execution of the King.

(To complete the story, I include a section of the poem

Chavenage, which the Lowsley-Williams family have kindly allowed me to print.)

When all his relations had assembled,
And their several well-known equipages
Were crowding the courtyard,
And the sick man was now breathing his last,
The household were surprised to observe that another
    coach,
Ornamented in even more than the gorgeous embell-
    ishments
Of that period, and drawn by black horses,
Was approaching the door of the vehicle in great
    solemnity.

When it had arrived, making a short stay,
The door of the vehicle opened in some unseen manner,
And clad in his shroud, the shade of the Colonel glided
Into the carriage, and the door instantly closing upon him,
The coach rapidly but silently withdrew from the House.

Not however, with such speed but there was time to
    perceive
That the driver was a beheaded man, that he was arrayed
In the royal vestments with the Garter moreover
On his leg, and that star of that illustrious order
Upon his breast. No sooner had the coach arrived
At the gateway of the manor-court than the whole
    appearance
Vanished in flames of fire.

The story further maintains that, to this day,
Every Lord of Chavenage, dying in the manor-house,
Takes his departure in this ominous conveyance.

Being unrelated to the unfortunate Colonel, the current owner is fairly certain that he will depart in a more conventional manner.

David Lowsley-Williams tells three stories of his own, which can't match the tale of Nathaniel for sheer supernatural terror, but are perhaps a little more plausible

I was doing a security tour of the bedrooms at Chavenage during a Hunt Dance, when I stumbled upon a couple cavorting in the Oliver Cromwell Room. I wasn't so greatly shocked by their antics, as the fact that they had chosen to perform them without taking a valuable silk cover off the bed first. People really should take their shoes off if they want to do these things. Anyway, I remonstrated with the lovers, and left the room.

Later, someone asked me to reveal the identity of the paramours. 'Actually, I kept my eyes fastened on the energetically humping nether cheeks, so I never saw their faces,' was my highly diplomatic reply.

Describing a family picture on a tour one day, I pointed out that the dog in it was an English Flat Coat Retriever, a breed which nearly died out when the Labrador became so popular. On saying this, a forthright lady cried out from the back of the group, 'What absolute nonsense!'

I turned to face the antagonist, and asked her how she could be so certain that I was wrong. 'I am the Secretary of the Flat Coat Society of Great Britain, that's how!' came the swift response. It just goes to show how careful a guide has got to be.

A feature of *Noel Edmonds' House Party* (along with the ubiquitous Mr Blobby, that monstrous piece of inflatable pink lard) is the 'Gotcha!' Awards. Here, a celebrity is lured into a suitable activity, only to be surprised by the bearded host, who just manages to control his fits of hysterics to interview the disconcerted guest, and present him with his prize. It's *This is Your Life* without the life.

Kriss Akabusi, a born-again Christian and accomplished 400-metre hurdler, was asked to take part in a documentary about the religious community surrounding Chavenage. He accepted the invitation, and on the appointed day arrived at the house to begin filming.

At the end of the scenes shot with him at Chavenage, he is cut short in his ruminations by the sight of a costume-clad Noel emerging from a folly at the far end of the garden. Enough to terrorize the hardiest of souls I should think, but Mr Akabusi took it in his stride – as you'd expect him to!

Rockingham in Northamptonshire, a castle built by William the Conqueror, was regularly used by early kings of England until the sixteenth century when it was granted to Edward Watson whose family still live there today.

In 1985, the BBC filmed a major Civil War series at Rockingham. One of the scenes had Prince Rupert bursting out of the front door, administering a passionate farewell embrace to the daughter of the house, leaping on to a horse and galloping out through the towers accompanied by his faithful poodle, Boy. Such is the stuff period drama thrives on.

Everything was ready for the first 'take' – horse held steady by the ostler, dog sitting obediently next to the horse, and young girl making final adjustments to her hair.

'Take One – ACTION!' The door crashes open, the Prince comes hurtling out, takes maiden in his arms, kisses her, then mounts the horse in one movement, and gallops off. Poodle watches the scene with interest but ignores his cue, preferring instead to give his underbelly a scratch. By this time, Rupert is long gone and the scene is ruined.

So they try it again. 'Take Two – ACTION!' Out comes Rupert, kiss kiss, one big leap and away he goes. Still no reaction from the poodle, who has located the irritating flea and is giving it a proper pawing. The director scowls; and the dog-handler turns a fierce eye to the dog. The dog looks back, blissfully unconcerned.

Once more. 'Take Three – ACTION!' This time the dog-handler tries to add an element of motivation, and at *le moment critique* begins to jump up and down, waving his arms at his charge in frantic shooing movements. The poodle watches the silent cabaret, yawns and lies back on its haunches observing its owner with a mixture of incredulity and boredom. But the director has had enough. He picks up a stone and hurls it at the uncooperative canine.

Canine clambers to its feet, stretches, and recognizing at last that some performance is required of it, strolls over to the camera and lifts its leg on the tripod. 'CUT!!!'

Michael Saunders-Watson of Rockingham rarely takes visitors round the castle. On one open day, however, he had to fill in for a guide who was sick. After a while, he began to have some difficulty in sticking to the text. Having to say the same thing over and over again – albeit to different people – is not easy, and the temptation to embellish can be great. In due course Michael succumbed.

Leading a party into the Tudor kitchen, he drew their attention to a sign on the door which reads: 'No person, whether belonging to the Family or not, is ever, under any pretext, to enter this place without obtaining leave.' Michael knew that an explanation was required, but not satisfied with the calibre of the truth, he embarked upon an amplification of his own.

'When I was a child,' he improvised, 'the cook was extremely fierce and extremely fat. She'd sit on the edge of the refectory table – you'll notice it's badly warped at one end – clasping a large rolling pin and bellowing at passers-by, and ruling the kitchen with a rod of iron. Terrifying woman … the sign is hers.'

'And when was that?' one of the group asked.

'Oh, it must have been 1937, or '38 – sometime before the war,' answered Michael, not too sure himself.

'For your information,' said the visitor, indignantly, 'my mother was cook here at that time, and I remember her distinctly as being petite, rather shy and mild. So what on earth are you talking about?'

The owner of Rockingham Castle is now a great deal more circumspect on his occasional guided tours.

From Julian Luttrell, formerly of Dunster, a thirteenth-century castle in Somerset, which was remodelled by Anthony Salvin in the nineteenth century, and is now owned and run by the National Trust

One day, in the summer before Dr Beeching's axe, my father was travelling between Dunster and London on the train. At that time he was a director of the Great Western Railway and made this journey regularly. In the compartment with him were two middle-aged ladies. They sat opposite each other by the window, and began a loud discussion on the merits of taking a holiday in the Minehead area, which they had evidently both just done.

My father had started reading his newspaper, when he overheard one of the ladies – which was hard not to do, as their voices were indeed sonorous – remarking to the other, 'Oh look! There's Dunster Castle! Did you manage to go round it this year?'

'No I didn't,' came the reply. 'I meant to, but on the day that I had planned to go, it poured with rain. So I did something else instead.'

'What a shame! It's quite lovely, you know. Wonderful views, lovely gardens, and heaps of foreign plants. That's why it's all so tragic,' and the woman let out a deep sigh.

My father couldn't help catching the resonance of this last sentence, and noting that the conversation seemed to have broken off rather abruptly, he glanced in curiosity over the top of his paper.

The woman in question had her index finger aimed at her temple and was rotating it suggestively. My father quickly understood what that suggestion was!

'There's a husband, a wife and two children. All the same apparently … Really such a tragedy.'

My father, with the news of his lunacy laid so starkly before him, gathered up the paper and returned to a perusal of the day's other 'exclusives'.

It seems to come as something of a shock for visitors to the castle when they find me, not in the expected ermine robes, but in rather dirty old corduroys and an open-necked shirt. It may account for the number of times that I am mistaken for one of the gardeners.

Some time back, just after my father died, I turned up expectantly at one o'clock for luncheon, only to be told by my mother that it would be late. She went on to point out that, whilst I was waiting, I could dead-head some of the roses that were badly needing attention. She would call me when the meal was ready to be served.

The castle opens its doors to the public at two o'clock, but the lady on the gate is so enthusiastic that she allows those who arrive ten minutes or so early to wander round the gardens. As I busied away with the 'Floribunda', I suddenly heard a strange voice at my side. 'What a lovely afternoon,' it said.

I looked up to find a florid gentleman of middle age, whom I assumed from his accent was on holiday from the Black Country. 'Yes it is,' I said.

'Nice place, wouldn't want to run it myself, mind – must cost a fortune.'

'Yes.'

'Erm … What's it like working here? Boss all right, is he?'

'Yes, she's very pleasant and cares a lot about the gardens,' I replied.

'You're lucky,' the garrulous gentleman exclaimed. 'Makes all the difference when the boss knows about his business.'

At this point my mother, unaware of the conversation taking place beneath her, opened the library window and called out to me, 'Aren't you coming in now, darling?'

I glanced at the visitor to gauge his reaction. He made no comment, but flashed a salacious grin. From his expression, he was clearly imagining an arrangement along the lines of *Lady Chatterley's Lover*. I was tempted to disabuse him of this inaccurate and unfortunate connotation, but chose instead to beat a hasty retreat.

Patrick, Earl of Lichfield, who lives at Shugborough in Staffordshire, remembers an incident which neatly captures the innocence (and insight) of children.

It is Christmas Day. Patrick, his sister and all the household staff are eagerly awaiting the entrance into the red drawing room of Father Christmas, who by tradition is always played by Great-Uncle Colonel Frederick Keppel. He is however so well disguised by the scarlet coat, complete with fluffy trimmings, and an enormous snow-white beard, that the Anson youngsters are comprehensively conned. They hold out their hands expectantly, as Santa distributes the presents to staff and family alike.

On receiving her small gift, Patrick's sister looks up into the giant beaming face and says: 'Thank you, Uncle Fred!'

Her grandmother, horrified, shrieks: 'But why do you suppose it's Uncle Fred, Elizabeth?'

'Because he smells of sherry – he always does!' she answers, her triumph complete.

Excerpt from a letter written by the Hon. Sir Steve Runciman to Patrick, Earl of Lichfield, 11 June 1973

The story of the origins of the word 'loo' was told me by The Duke of Buccleuch's aunt, Lady Constance Cairns. Your relations feature largely in it.

In 1867 when the 1st Duke of Abercorn was Viceroy of Ireland there was a large houseparty at Viceregal Lodge, and amongst the guests were the Lord Lieutenant of County Roscommon, Mr Edward King Tennison, and his wife Lady Louisa, daughter of The Earl of Lichfield.

Lady Louisa was, it seems, not very lovable; and the two youngest Abercorn sons, Lord Frederick and Lord Ernest, took her namecard from her bedroom door and placed it on the door of the only WC in the guest wing. So in those select ducal circles everyone became familiar – Jimmy Abercorn told me that when he was a boy one went to the Lady Lou (though he never told me who Her Ladyship was).

Now in these democratic days the courtesy title has been dropped, and within the last thirty years or so – only really since the war – the term has seeped down into middle-class and working-class usage. But it all really originates from your Hamilton uncles being ungallant to your Anson aunt; who I think should have her immortality recognized.

According to the Viscount Bridgeman (a distant cousin, whom I refer to as 'My Noble Kinsman', when we're in the Chamber of the House of Lords together), a noble Lord dreamt that he was addressing their Lordships' house, and when he woke up, he was!

Here's another story from Viscount Bridgeman

A peer succeeded a cousin when well into his eighties. He arrived at the House of Lords to take his seat, and announced to Red Coat, who was opening the door to his taxi, 'I've come for my christening!'

His wife, sensing that an explanation was called for, stepped forward and said to Red Coat, 'I'm afraid that his Lordship hasn't been very well lately and is a little bit tired.'

To which Red Coat is reported to have replied, 'Oh don't

worry, my Lady, we get them much worse than this!'

Benjamin Disraeli was a frequent visitor to Weston Park. The visits weren't so much inspired by a desire to view the house, as an inordinate and extravagant fondness for my great-great-grandmother, Selina, 3rd Countess of Bradford. She was flattered by his attentions, of course, but also found them somewhat embarrassing. This might have had something to do with her age – she was in her late fifties – but probably owed more to the fact that she was perfectly happily married at the time. Disraeli remained undeterred though, and launched a campaign of adoration that lasted many years.

His devotion was unflagging. He wrote some 1,100 letters to her – at the staggering rate of three or four a week – most of which were composed during his prime ministership. He even penned letters to her from the official state stagecoach, whilst hurrying to keep appointments with the Queen.

His greatest bid for Selina's affections came when he proposed to her sister, Lady Chesterfield, which may seem a strange way of going about things, except that such a marriage would inevitably have led to more time being spent in the company of his true love. Sadly neither scheme worked: the proposal was turned down, and his friendship with the Countess never went beyond the platonic. Disraeli was evidently more successful with matters of State, than those of the heart.

But we must be grateful for his prolific correspondence. All the letters he sent are still kept at Weston. Edged in black, in memory of his late wife, they reveal a fascinating insight into his character, and other notable figures of the age. He often mentions Queen Victoria, for instance, who is quite casually referred to as 'the Faerie', as in, 'Today the Faerie was in Seventh Heaven having received a letter of felicitations from the King of the Belges.'

Politics comes in for light comment. He reserves his energies for the description of social events, in which he shows characteristic wit, and not a little sarcasm.

On a visit to Sandringham in 1875, Disraeli refers to some of the guests as 'Nameless toadies in the shape of mysterious Polish Counts'. Another unfortunate individual is compared to 'Lazarus in Sebastian del Piombo's picture, save that he seems like the one to be consigned to the tomb, instead of emerging from one'. Perhaps it wasn't a very good bash.

He also had very decided views on the quality and presentation of food, stating: 'I don't at all mind a bad dinner because I make a rule never to eat it.'

At a disastrous supper with the German Ambassador in 1876, he encountered 'A wondrous dish of salmon, that should have been condemned at Billingsgate as unfit for human food'!

On the same evening he was forced to sit between 'Lady Derby and Constance who hate each other and who both, in their time, had confidentially imparted this reciprocity of amiable sentiment to me.' He goes on, 'The dinner was something unearthly – impossible to conceive so many dark, hard dishes could have been collected and what cooks of Pandemonium could have prepared them.' He plainly had the knack of turning up at the wrong parties ...

It might have been this that drove him to seek isolation, for despite his elevated position, he spent many solitary hours at Hughenden, his country mansion in Buckinghamshire. There he kept peacocks of which he was very fond. You can hear the ring of affection in these, his words to Selina: 'The peacocks are still moulting. They have no tails and persist in showing themselves like Falstaff's ragged regiment. They have eaten all the flowers and have no beauty to substitute for that which they have destroyed.' Cherished pets, then ...

He once gave the Countess the unusual present of a yellow parrot – 'The Parrot with his Golden Robes', as he called it. If this was a last desperate attempt to win her heart, the bird bribe failed to pay off. Still, my great-great-grandmother kept the parrot, which sat in the Orangery for some twenty-five years. It was always presumed to be a cock bird because of its highly distinctive plumage, but one morning it quite suddenly, and to everyone's surprise, started to lay eggs, at the rate of one per day for twenty-three days. The parrot seemed equally mystified by its new-found talent (and gender); perhaps the shock was too much, because on the twenty-fourth day it keeled over and died.

It was then stuffed and put on display at Weston in a glass case, where it can be seen today, with the fruits of its labour resting in a little wooden box on top. The parrot still looks amazed!

But it is, no doubt, a notable addition to what Disraeli described as 'Weston's scenes so fair'.

The story of the parrot holds a tremendous fascination for many of the 10,000 schoolchildren who visit Weston every year. We provide a special tour for them which is tailored around things they will find interesting like a stuffed parrot, or a secret door. Too much family history or long art lectures would merely bore them, and as we all know, with little boys and girls boredom generally spells trouble!

Some of the children are so moved by their experiences at Weston Park, that they take the time to write thank you letters, addressed personally to me. Or, more accurately, they are ordered to do so by their teacher or Brownie leader as part of a class project. The resulting epistles are often amusing in their abruptness, refreshing in their honesty, and occasionally shocking in their critical judgement. But I always read them with pleasure, and have included a selection on pages 72–5.

From Gyles Brandreth, MP for the City of Chester, former TV-am presenter and wearer of funny sweaters

My father used to say that when he was elevated to the peerage he would change his name to Lovaduck, so that when he came into a room, people would cry, 'Oh Lord Lovaduck!'

I have had the pleasure – and the privilege – of meeting quite a number of lords and the lordlier they are the more I like them. My one regret is that I never met the lordliest lord of them all, the first Marquess Curzon of Kedleston.

George Nathaniel Curzon was a Tory grandee of the old school. Viceroy of India, Foreign Secretary and, very possibly, had he not been in the House of Lords, Prime Minister instead of Stanley Baldwin in 1923. He had the Grand Manner; his style was evident even as an undergraduate:

My name is George Nathaniel Curzon,
I am a most superior person.
My cheeks are pink, my hair is sleek,
I dine at Blenheim once a week.

Not for Curzon the classless society. For a number of years he was Chancellor of Oxford University and when, in 1921, Queen Mary was to be entertained at his college, Balliol, he was asked to approve the proposed menu in advance. He returned it to the Bursar with the single comment: 'Gentlemen do not take soup at luncheon.'

One evening, a little before the outbreak of the Great War,

Sir John Offley School
Madeley,
Greve,
24th June

Dear Lord and Lady Bradford,
One Tuesday mrs williams and class
six went to weston park but it
was very wet but all class six
still enjoyed it even the
people who were sick on the
way. I think that the aquar-
ium was nice I liked it
because of all the different
shapes and sizes of the
fish and rocks and I
liked the live coral I am
Glad it was not dead because

I like nature I like live
things not dead things.
I thought that the things in
the house were nice but I
did not like the dead parot
it was horbel because. I like
birds I am a bird watcher
that's why I dont like the
dead parot. I liked the
plate with a green finch
and a bull finch on it.
I liked the tapestries to
they were very very nice.
I liked the gold on the foot
I would not have liked to
live or own the house I
think it is to posh for me.
yours sincerely David Bradley

Brom ford Junior
School
Brom ford Road
Hodge Hill
Birming Ham
8th July

Thursday

Dear Earl and Countess of
Bradford

When we went to Western Park
I went on the Adventure Play ground
I was very happy and I went Down
The Slid and I went on the Bridgers
and I went Down The Pole and I
went on the scramal net and I got
out stuck and I could I could not
get out of the Scramble net and we
we went to the house and I Saw
a Bird and it had alt eggs
and they stuffed The Bird with
fur Wes the colours your
sincerely

Steve Finlan

Class LCR
Ravensmed CP School,
Bignall End,
Stoke-on-Trent,
Staffs.
20th July

Dear Guide
Thank-you very much for exsplaining
everything to us. I enjoyed it very much. I liked
the parrot and the eggs. Where did the parrots
go out of the eggs? I liked the secret door.
Yours Sincerely
Susan Brossington

Bishop Bridgeman C of E primary school
Rupert Street,
Bolton
16th June

My Lord
    I just wanted to say thank you
for letting us come into the private part
of the house.
It was very nice.
The Temple of Diana was nice too
everything was nice.
I hope you and your wife had a lovely
time on your holiday.
I hope it was fine for you.
I hope we can go next year and see the
house again.
Although it was raining we still had
a good time we went on the adventure
playground it was very good but
when I went down the slide I landed

in a little pool of water.
I enjoyed it very much.
The paintings were very nice and all
the rooms were beautiful.
We saw paintings of girls and boys
in old clothes.
The tapestry room was very beautiful.
If I lived at Weston park I would get
lost because it is a big house.
Thank you for leaving a letter telling
the guides to look after us and telling
us about you and the rooms.
I have the honour to remain
your Lordship's obedient servant.
    Sharon Tuff.

1st Church Aston Brownies

Dear Lord Bradford,
Sorry I didn't come to Western Park it was because I was at my Aunty Deas I'm sure I would have enjoyed it very much And I'm hoping to come next time

Love
Sarah
Cotton

1st church Aston Brownies

Dear Lord Bradford,
I enjoyed It very much. I liked the Adventure play ground and the house best. I don't like fish but I liked the aqurium. I bought a 80p Shell doll. I think I enjoyed It best because it rained I enjoyed every minuet.

Love
Donna Hesbrook
x x x x x x x x x

1st church Aston Brownies

Dear
Lord Bradford I am wrighting to say I liked it when I went I have been on holiday for a fortnight I hope You are having a lovely time I have started an new class at school I am a 3rd year

Love from
Sarah N

1st church Aston
Dear Lord Bradford
I did not come to weton park becaues I whent on holiday to harlech.

Love
fome Vicky

he and a friend were strolling down Regent Street when they came upon the window of Garrards, the jewellers. They paused to take in the range of gold and silverware on display and Curzon's eye was caught by a small silver cylindrical object nestling on a tiny blue cushion at the rear of the window. 'What's that?' he asked his companion.

'What?'

'That, up there,' said Curzon, pointing at the piece of silver.

'Why, Curzon,' said his friend, 'that's a napkin ring.'

'What on earth is a "napkin ring"?' enquired Curzon.

'Surely you've come across a napkin ring before now, Curzon?'

'No, no, truly, I haven't. Pray, what does it do?'

'Well,' said his companion, 'there are some people who cannot afford fresh linen at every meal, so that after breakfast they will take their napkin and fold it not once, but twice, and then roll it into a tube and insert the napkin into that silver ring to keep the same napkin to use again at luncheon.'

Curzon shook his head, sighed and gazed intently at the little silver napkin ring. 'Can there really be *such* poverty?'

The 8th Marquess of Hertford opened Ragley Hall in Warwickshire in 1958. It is one of England's finest Palladian country mansions, and was designed by Robert Hooke in the late seventeenth century.

Hugh Hertford and his wife did most of the work themselves in the early stages, as they had very few staff. This included a walk round the home farm at the crack of dawn, a drive in the mini-bus to collect the daily cleaners (none of them had cars in those days and they found the prospect of the walk from the main lodge gates to the house rather a daunting one: it's a mile and a half long and uphill all the way), and a morning spent running between the farm and the estate office. Then Hugh would drive the cleaners home, pick up the guides, and finally embark upon an afternoon's salesmanship – sitting in his farmer's jeans, the Marquess could be found touting the Ragley *Guide Book* to the visitors, none of whom recognized the slightly grubby figure at the desk.

On one occasion, he was sitting there as usual in an especially dilapidated pair of denims, when an elderly gentleman paused over the desk and commented, 'Such a pity nobody can afford to live in these houses any more.'

To which Lord Hertford replied, 'But I do live here!'

'Yes,' said the man thoughtfully. 'Such a pity, such a pity …'

The Marquess has been known to complain that people never look him in the face when they are making a purchase. He observes that middle- and upper-class visitors are particularly unkindly, and tend to peer straight over his head. But one afternoon, after several hours of repeating 'Good afternoon. Would you like to buy a guide book?', the Marquess became a little *laissez-faire* himself. The strain of the hard sell must have taken its toll – he began to pay increasingly less attention to the customer, and more to his navel, until he was roused from his reveries by a familiar though resentful voice. He looked up to see that he had offered a guide book to his own mother, and had one hand extended, expecting payment. As he says, 'She was really quite cross.'

I have already mentioned the secret door. This is to be found at the far end of the library, and is disguised as a bookcase, similar to the ones that line the whole room. In this particular one though there is a catch, which opens up the section into another room, allowing you to leave the library in style. It was created during the reign of Queen Victoria, when many of the rooms at Weston were, at considerable expense I suspect, switched around; what is now the front hall, for instance, used to be the library. Maybe the owners spent rather too much money, and the secret opening was in fact part of a highly sophisticated network of tunnels and phoney passages built to aid rapid and invisible escape from the creditors. If this is the case, I have yet to discover the rest of the network, but I'm still trying!

The family must have had lots of fun thinking up imaginative titles for the spines of the fake books that line the secret doorway. Some of these are pretty obvious, like *How to Stop a Gap*, or *The Library of Useless Knowledge* (in twelve volumes). Others are a little more subtle, *Stage Coaches versus Steam Coaches*, *The American Peerage*, *Parvum in Multo*; others absurd, *Transactions of the Toxopholite Society* (in twelve volumes), *Debates in the Eskimaux Parliament*; the majority are simply obscure, for instance, *Cobbett on Consistency*. I mean, who on earth was Cobbett, and why was he so obsessed with consistency? Whoever he was I'll lay a bet he wasn't very consistent. The most interesting ones are those that have been overtaken by the march of science and technology. *Legends of the Thames Tunnel* and *Voyage to the Moon* must have appeared unlikely enough to amuse the Victorians.

Sudeley Castle in Gloucestershire, one of England's most charming and unusual country houses, which was the inspiration for 'Blandings' in P.G. Wodehouse's novels, is the home of Lord and Lady Ashcombe, their family, and many unusual animals.

Lady Ashcombe remembers an unfortunate incident with a

*Scottish visitor, which followed the fairly recent addition to the
household of an exuberant and deeply mischievous Samoyed*

At six months our Samoyed, Zabik, had developed into a
large bundle of white fur, with a penchant for chewing fine
fabrics. One warm autumn afternoon, we were outside
enjoying a game of tug of war, when at the far end of the
garden appeared a distinguished looking Scotsman dressed in
an elegant kilt. Studiously absorbed in his guide book, he did
not notice Zabik come bounding across the lawn towards
him, until it was too late. By that time, the Samoyed had sunk
his teeth into the tartan delicacy, and was yanking at it in the
manner we had been playing.

When I arrived on the scene, I realized that the Scotsman
was not in sporting mood. Wrestling with an over-assertive
sledge-dog was perhaps not his idea of a good day out, and to
be sure there was no mention of it in the guide book.

After a prolonged and embarrassing struggle on my knees,
I finally extracted Zabik's sharp teeth from the material. It
was then my turn to retreat, offering sincerest apologies for
my pet's behaviour, and noticing as I did so that a sizeable
chunk of the Scotsman's kilt was missing.

Missing but not lost – there seemed to be something
colourful hanging out of the side of the Samoyed's mouth. I
thought it best not to draw attention to the gentleman's now
flawed attire. I was still counting on the fact that the visitor
hadn't recognized me as the mistress of the house ...

From Derek Nimmo

A tale which I have always rather treasured was told to me
by the Hon. William Douglas-Home. William and Brian
Johnston had been at Eton together. Soon after they had left,

Brian, hearing that William was staying at Brown's Hotel, decided to collect him and, inevitably, take him off to Lord's for a Test Match.

When Brian arrived, he greeted William and, hearing the news that William's mother, Lady Home, was also staying in the hotel, he asked for her room number. '210,' replied William.

Brian bounded up the stairs to pay his respects to William's Ma. He knocked at the door. 'Come in,' said Lady Home.

When Brian entered, Lady Home was sitting naked in front of the dressing table. 'How dare you, Brian,' she exclaimed.

'But you said, "come in".'

'Yes, I know,' said Lady Home, 'but I thought you were a waiter!'

Another incident, of a theatrical nature this time, happened many years ago when I was appearing in repertory in Clacton-on-Sea, where we had a Maltese scenic artist. Now Maltese scenic artists are fairly thin on the ground, and equally thin was his command of the English language.

The play we were doing at the time was Terence Rattigan's *The Deep Blue Sea*. In it was required a painting of Weymouth pier. The scenic artist was asked to produce such a picture.

Came the dress rehearsal, and we were surprised to find in the centre of the set, instead of a marine landscape, an elaborately painted representation of an old buffer, complete with moustache, coronation robes and coronet, and a little sign underneath which read, Lord Weymouth.

In less enlightened times, a forebear of Charles Clive-Ponsonby-Fane was invited to speak as guest of honour at a smart London dinner. The night of the function arrived and as he made his way to the High Table, he straightened his tie, made final mental corrections to his speech, and took his seat feeling comfortable and assured.

He looked to his left, smiled urbanely at his neighbour, a ruddy-faced military type, then turned to his right to repeat the process. He was met with the distinctive features and steady gaze of an Oriental gentleman. Time stood still for several seconds – the Chinaman continued to stare impassively as Charles's grandfather racked his brains for a suitable phrase of conversational Mandarin. As the soup arrived he toyed with the idea of feigning a respiratory attack, but suddenly inspiration struck and pointing to the mock turtle soup, he asked in his best Chinese: 'Likee soupee?'

'Velly muchee,' came the grinning reply, accompanied by a vigorous nodding of the head.

The crushing silence resumed – right through until the arrival of the next course, when desperation and politeness forced a similar inquiry: 'Likee fishee?'

'Velly muchee!'

At last it was time for the speech, which the guest of honour delivered at considerable length. Eventually, he sat down pleased with the way that the power and resonance of his words had induced a state of semi-hypnosis among the listeners. Many were so captivated that they completely forgot to applaud, he noted with pride. His satisfaction was swiftly banished, however, by the sight of the Chinaman being introduced as the final speaker of the evening. He felt slighted but also acutely embarrassed at the prospect of a stuttering, barely comprehensible dissertation on the finer points of Eastern philosophy.

To his shock and growing shame he listened as his Chinese friend began speaking in the most beautiful English and gave a speech which skipped delicately and expertly along a series of absorbing topics. The orator told some excellent jokes, alluded effortlessly to Virgil, Homer and Milton, and even ended with a risqué tale about George Bernard Shaw related in a faultless Irish brogue – all in under twenty minutes.

After the rapturous applause had subsided, the Chinaman turned to Charles's gobsmacked grandfather and quietly asked: 'Likee speechee?'

Gaulden, a red sandstone manor house in Somerset was occupied for over 200 years by the Turberville family, whom Thomas Hardy immortalized in the novel *Tess of the d'Urbervilles*. Now it is a genuine 'lived-in-home' from where James Starkie, the present owner, recounts a story from the days before the advent of British Telecom, when the Post Office installed a luminous red telephone in the Starkies' bedroom. It looked somewhat incongruous alongside the Jacobean four-poster and the other period decorations. So much so that, before visitors started arriving, James usually tucked the telephone under the bed.

However, some time after installation, James's wife was leading a party along the top landing, when the wretched thing began to ring. This was most inconvenient, but as luck would have it, her husband was nearby. He rushed to pull the plug out of the socket, before the party could get as far as the bedroom.

For some reason best known to himself, James decided to answer the call. Despite this act of lunacy, all would have been well, if the caller had not turned out to be an especially long-winded, military type, who seemed to have some difficulty with the construction of sentences.

James's spouse, oblivious to her partner's problem, heard the ringing stop and, assuming everything was in order, ushered the visitors into their chamber.

The party was met by the unedifying spectacle of James Starkie, owner of Gaulden Manor, his head and shoulders wedged under the valance, and his backside stuck up in the air. He was mumbling away, obviously in some discomfort: 'Oh yes, General ... Of course I will, General ... Tell me more, General.'

This was enough to cause considerable embarrassment, and not a few titters. James's wife thought it best to lead the party into another section of the house as quickly as possible.

From Holkham Hall in Norfolk, ancestral home to the Earls of Leicester comes a story featuring Lady Carey Coke. At a wedding reception, Lady Coke (pronounced 'Cook') was engaged in conversation by a young woman, who asked, 'What is your name?' Lady Carey replied, 'I am a Coke from Holkham.' The young woman said, 'Oh, that's nice, I'm a maid from Yorkshire.'

The 2nd Earl of Leicester was taking a stroll around the lake and encountered a young nanny with a baby in a pram. He stopped and asked her, 'And who is the father of this jolly little chap?' To which she replied, 'You are, my Lord.'

In one of the grandest bedrooms at Weston, there hangs a magnificent painting by Sir Peter Lely. It is a portrait of the Earl of Dysart, who married one of the three daughters of Lady Wilbraham, foundress of Weston Park. Most experts agree that it is a supreme example of Lely's skills, and you don't have to be a connoisseur of fine art to see why.

The subject is captured brilliantly – Dysart was plainly a

good-looking man and the sort who knows it only too well. He sits smouldering on a chair, a far-away look in his eyes, with a bearing that would seem to say: 'Yes, I know I'm gorgeous, but do I really have to pose for this picture any longer? Womankind anxiously awaits my return.'

Another striking feature of the picture is that, wherever you are in the room, Dysart is watching you. This can be more than a little unsettling, particularly for our female guests. If you can imagine being scrutinized by a cross between Lord Byron and Jack Nicholson, you will understand the problem. Quite apart from the fact that the rakish Earl appears to be mentally undressing you from the minute that you enter the room, you soon realize that no part of the chamber is safe from his libidinous attentions – he sees everything.

When my sister-in-law came to stay for the first time at the sensitive age of thirteen, she was put in the Dysart Room, and became so distressed by the leering portrait that she took the drastic action of hiding in the cupboard. This seemed to be the only way to combat the voyeuristic tendencies of an unmistakable womanizer, and to undress in comfort. Leaving the closet door partly ajar, she found that there was just enough space to disrobe. With the lights turned off, she'd scramble from the cupboard to the bed, and pull the covers tightly over her head, thereby denying the lascivious one the pleasure of seeing her as nature intended.

It is a testament to Lely's powers of re-creation, that his painting can force a teenage girl into this, the strangest of bedtime rituals. I very much doubt that a lesser artist would have had the same effect.

Beaulieu Abbey, situated in the beautiful New Forest between Bournemouth and Southampton, was founded in 1204, and though many of the buildings were destroyed in the

Dissolution, much of beauty and interest remains, including the Domus which houses an exhibition of medieval monastic life. It has been Lord Montagu's family home since 1538, and is now most famous for the National Motor Museum, set up in the grounds by the present Lord Montagu.

When the first few private houses opened to the public, it generated an extraordinary amount of popular interest and a corresponding response from the press. Suddenly, faces that had only graced the pages of the upmarket glossy magazines were splashed across more humble newsprint.

One evening a group of owners emerged from a meeting in central London and hailed a taxi. As they climbed aboard, the driver of the cab took a good look at one of them. "Ere mate, don't I know your face?'

'My name is Bedford, from Woburn,' responded the Duke of Bedford.

On hearing that, the driver burst into peels of merry laughter. 'That's a good one, mate,' he chortled. 'If you're the Duke of Bedford, then I'm Lord Montagu!'

Whereupon there was a sharp tap on his shoulder. 'Not so, *I'm* Lord Montagu!'

When Lord Montagu was trying to promote his sales of wine, he received a letter from the Beaulieu vineyard in California, asking him to stop using their name. He replied that since the Beaulieu Abbey monks planted their first vines at the beginning of the thirteenth century, he had a slightly older claim on the name than they did. After this, the correspondence mysteriously dried up.

The business of stately homes is fiercely competitive; industrial espionage is not unheard of.

In the mid 60s, Lord Bath made several attempts to enter Beaulieu incognito, in order to assess the strengths of the opposition. He tried to pass as a paying visitor, but one long-serving lady on the desk always recognized him. In fact it was remarkably easy to do so, as he would unfailingly sport a red-spotted handkerchief in his breast pocket. He seemed oblivious to the benefits a disguise would have on his spying activities. The lady alerted Lord Montagu every time, and the owner would pop out to meet the undercover agent. 'Damn!' Lord Bath would cry. 'I can never get past that blasted woman without her noticing!'

From Jean Starkie, of Gaulden Manor, in Somerset

I have noticed that real experts tend to be modest people and reluctant to boast about their favourite subjects. So, whenever I see someone taking a detailed interest in a particular object, I will always talk to them in the hope of hearing something new. Over the years I have learned an enormous amount about our many possessions in this way.

One day, a couple paid to come in on the dot of two o'clock, just as we opened. (I wanted to be around the house because a large party of the local townswomen's guild was also booked to arrive.) As the moments ticked by, I noticed the husband peering studiously at our old Welsh dresser which stands in the hall. 'Aha,' I thought. 'An expert!'

But as I went over to have a chat, he dropped on to his knees and started to scramble about on all fours. In a temporary break from sanity, I decided that he must have lost one of his contact lenses, so I joined him on the floor, saying consolingly, 'Don't worry, I'll give you a hand.'

The man looked at me as though I'd offered to shoot him. Whilst I poked about frantically under the dresser, he got to his feet and, with his wife, left the room.

Meanwhile, I continued the search, and all might have been well had not the good ladies from the townswomen's guild chosen that precise moment to walk in through the door. I think they were a little concerned to see a supine mistress of the house, fiddling about on the floor, and muttering strange incantations under her breath: 'Where are you, my precious? Reveal yourself!'

To make matters worse, I later found out that the offended husband was indeed an expert, a connoisseur no less, and had been checking the legs of the dresser merely to see if they were genuine. I can only assume that he fled in embarrassment at my extraordinary antics under the furniture.

Sir Nicholas Fairbairn – a personal view

I begin this anecdotal vignette by marvelling at the wonders of our Post Office and its special and affectionate staff. I received a letter merely addressed to Mr Fairbairn, Scotland, but they divined its destination and delivered it to me.

My drive is kept in such a condition that it is intended to keep intruders out, but they never complain. They once delivered a packet containing stinking human excreta, addressed to my wife and comparing its contents to myself. Bravo those who serve us so faithfully and courteously.

Our house, built in 1210, was for some time, though not originally, occupied by the Hendersons of Fordell, who have had the arrogance to assume that it is their personal fiefdom. Accordingly they consider it a matter of right to invade our estate and even to demand, yes demand, access to the castle and 'appropriate' entertainment – by which they mean a dram. Well there is appropriate entertainment for them here, since Hugh de Camera who built the castle installed an *oubliette* and the Hendersons collected instruments of torture. Unfortunately in this sociological age, their use would be charged as criminal, however justified.

Once, when we were putting on a fête for charity, we were telephoned by some fellow at 6 a.m. – at a time when we were engaged in intimate matters – to ask if there was a 'white elephant' at the fête. I confirmed there was and resumed more pleasant indulgences.

Some years ago, I was defending a fellow on trial for his second consecutive charge of capital murder. I foolishly made a mistake that I have never made before or since.

I went to see him in his cell while the jury were out and he paid me the only compliment that I have ever received from a client. He said, 'Thank you very much, sir; thank you very much. I thought for one minute when you wis addressing the jury there, that I hadnae dunnit masel.' He was acquitted.

We once travelled to Florence years ago with Sir Ilay Campbell of Succoth, Bt, and Lady Campbell and after a refreshing and indulgent two weeks, we returned with a Parma ham proffered by our hotel. Despite being only about an eighth of the original, we could hardly carry it because it was so heavy. We staggered through the airports with it and divided it in two, our precious gourmet cargo. Unfortunately our rather glaikit maid thought it was steak and cut it into cubes and stewed it. *Sic transit gloriosus porcus.*

While on the subject of pigs, I should mention other pigs;

people who dump beds and 'suites' in the woods, people who poach or shoot on your property and people who despoil trees and features. They should be put down a coal mine for all time coming.

I have twice had the necessity of dismissing uninvited guests, brought by invited friends, from dining-room table and the castle for bad manners and insult. Why not? To tolerate intolerable behaviour destroys tolerance.

But in contrast, there are happy things, people who love to walk their dogs in the woods, ride in the estate and who love and admire the gardens; people who are helpful and loving in many ways; people who have contributed to the restoration of the castle with their skills. Good folk. Hurrah for love and excellence.

Eighteen years ago I received a letter from Oxfam, asking me to contribute to a book that they were producing entitled *Pass the Port*. Not the serious tome you might expect from a distinguished charity organization perhaps, but instead a compilation of after dinner jokes.

The Bumper Book of Oxfam Jokes? It sounded a little unlikely, I must admit. Still, it was all bona fide, and as for once I wasn't being asked for money, I decided to send them an Irish joke. Now I realize that in these days of high tolerance (or should that be high intolerance?), telling an Irish joke is a quick way to get yourself hauled up before the magistrates on a charge of spreading racist propaganda. But at the time, which was 1976, humour hadn't yet been institutionalized, and I didn't really need to ponder the possible ramifications of my comedy. So I submitted this:

An Irish Catholic girl goes to confession: 'Father, I've sinned grievously,' she tells the priest.

'Go on, my child,' he says.

'On Monday night I slept with Mick. On Tuesday night I slept with Sean. On Wednesday night I slept with Paddy. Oh Father, what shall I do?'

'Go home, my child, squeeze the juice from a whole lemon and drink it.'

'Oh Father, Father, will this purge me of my sin?'

'No, child. But it might take the smile off your face.'

However, unknown to me, my father had also been asked to send in a story; his too had a distinctly Irish flavour:

An Irish Catholic girl in Birmingham is visited by her local priest, who says: 'When you and your husband got married seven years ago, I knew you were good Catholics. You had one child in the first year, another the next year, but since then you've not had any more.'

'Well, Father, as you say, my husband and I are very good Catholics, and we had one child in the year after we married, and another child the next year, but then, Father, I read in the local newspaper that every third child born in Birmingham is black.'

Ahem ... even in the 1970s this might have raised a few eyebrows. But if the world wishes to label the Bradfords as being down on Ireland, they should go ahead. Just bear in mind that my mother was 100 per cent Irish herself and that she never had any problem with my father's sense of humour!

A problem facing many landowners in scenic areas of Britain is that of trespassing caravanners who, as a breed, seem to have no understanding of the sanctity of private property. In the north of Scotland the difficulties are especially acute, as little provision is made for their overnight parking requirements.

James Clark, son of Alan Clark (former Conservative

Defence Minister, diarist, media celebrity and owner of a wonderful castle in Kent), has a novel way of dealing with those travellers who intrude on to their large Sutherland estate. The Clarks are a family who never do things by halves, and James is no exception. Conceiving of a radical deterrent to the invading holidaymakers, he went out and bought a brand-new JCB digger.

That night he slipped out, and having spotted an errant caravan, dug a large trench around it. When the occupant woke up the following morning, he discovered that, for the time being anyway, his roaming activities had been severely restricted.

Later that day James received a call from the local policeman. It went something like this: 'Can I speak to Master James, please?'

'James Clark speaking.'

'Master James, it's Sergeant Wilson here.'

'Yes, Sergeant. What can I do for you?'

'Weell, Master James. Were ye oot last night?'

'What do you mean, Sergeant?'

'Weell, we seem to have a slight difficulty with a caravanner. The owner went to sleep peacefully last night, but when he woke up there was a huge trench aroond his vehicle. He couldn'a get away this morning until somebody filled it in. Yer wouldn'a know anything aboot this?'

'No, Sergeant. What a terrible inconvenience for him.'

'Weell, I just thought ye might know something aboot it.'

'I'll certainly keep my eyes open for anything, Sergeant.'

'Weell, thank you, Master James. Can I just suggest one thing?'

'Certainly, Sergeant.'

'Maybe it might be a guid idea to keep yer JCB in the garage from now on.'

A tale of terror and tragedy ... The Dodingtons who built Breamore in Hampshire were an unlucky couple: William the husband committed suicide in London in 1600, and his widow was murdered by their son in the house shortly after.

A portrait of the unfortunate woman hangs in Great Hall. Her ghost is said to appear on the impending death of the owner (at present Sir Westrow Hulse, who, owing to good health, cannot confirm the rumour) and to curse anyone who incurs her displeasure. One man who took the picture down to dust it, and was rudely dismissive of her capacity to haunt, fell off a ladder a few days later and died.

For their own good then, visitors are asked to respect the powers of the undead.

And a tale of titillation ... Lost Property: September 1993. A pair of lacy French knickers found in the drive leading up to the house. Visitors are reminded to keep an eye on their possessions at all times, as the owners cannot accept responsibility for missing underwear.

From the 11th Duke of Northumberland

In Surrey, they often call valleys 'bottoms'. My father, the 10th Duke, used to tell the amusing story of a valley on his Surrey estate. It had the charming name of 'Keeper's Bottom'.

In the 1920s an uncle of my father's was touring the Albury estate when, looking across, he noticed a good deal of movement in the valley. He became very excited and drove speedily down to Albury House. Reaching it, he shouted out: 'Georgie, Hugh, come quickly; there are hares all over the Keeper's Bottom!'

Staff

'You just can't get staff these days' – a cliché in our era, but probably an apposite one for my ancestor the 1st Countess of Bradford who, in 1824, was compelled to dismiss the house steward after a catalogue of swindles, embezzlements and sexual assaults came to her notice. At the time she described William Dunfee as 'the greatest hypocrite, the most [self-] interested being and the most immoral one that I have ever heard of'. What had he done to deserve this harsh judgement? Staffordshire archivists dealing with the period think they have the answer.

Dunfee was a past master at abusing his position in the household. Not content with prising 'commission' out of the local tradesfolk who supplied Weston Park, he clearly padded the bills to his own advantage, whilst accusing the other servants in the house of doing the same thing. He claimed for instance that Mrs Rotheram, Lady Bradford's valued housekeeper, made many a shilling by charging for eggs and muffins she hadn't received. Clearly a malcontent, Dunfee caused friction in the servants' hall, insinuating that Lord and Lady Bradford disliked certain of them, when he had no evidence of the kind. Furthermore he grumbled constantly that the family were ungenerous in giving him 'presents'. His boast that he only attended church for the sake of appearances did not go down at all well with Lady Bradford who was a staunch Anglican.

Dunfee's chief crime, however, was his avid pursuit of local girls and young married women on the estate. His reputation as a womanizer was widespread in the district. The poultry girl at Weston Park was his principal victim – he was said to be 'constantly after her' and, on at least one occasion, attacked her violently in the mangling room. Eventually Kitty, the poultry woman, felt obliged to dismiss the girl 'to keep her out of danger'. As well as the mangling room, Dunfee also favoured the broom cupboard as a suitable lair for his amorous activities. He had a penchant for married women since, in their case, any consequences of his actions 'would not signify'.

As a final flourish, and on his enforced departure from Weston, the dishonest steward 'was away before daylight, carrying off a cart load of luggage, amongst which were a dressing table, a washing table, and a supper tray'. Suffice to say, these articles were not his to carry anywhere.

It says much for Lady Bradford's generosity of spirit that despite Dunfee's many faults, she was able to recognize his talents, though sadly he "was not the good [servant] we thought he was." '

Who am I to argue with the historians?

Arley Hall, in Cheshire, is an example of the Victorian Jacobean style, set in twelve acres of beautiful, some might say peerless, gardens. The house was built by the owner's (The Hon. Michael Flower) great-great-grandfather in 1840.

Lord Ashbrook, Michael's father, is another example of one who made the difficult transgressional step from proprietor to guide. And like many, he learned to take the rough with the smooth.

After an extended tour of Arley, the peer led his group into the fine Salvin Chapel where he launched into a full dissertation on the building's architectural and historical pedigree. To say the talk was comprehensive is to understate the case. Enthusiastic to the end, the guide delivered an exhaustive exposition that left no nook, and scarcely a cranny, undiscovered or undescribed. Reaching the end of his treatise, Lord Ashbrook paused for breath, then enquired with the eagerness of a junior master: 'Are there any questions?'

Silence ... then more silence. The guide looked round the faces, his expression one of benevolent encouragement. As the hush continued, signs of desperation began to show – a twitch of the eye, a quiver of the lip, frantic rubbing of hands – all incipient signs of stress and acute embarrassment. But at last, a hand went up from the midst of the group.

'Yes, of course,' beamed the Lord, relief and gratitude flooding through his arteries, 'How can I help you?'

'Er, excuse me,' said a bored voice, 'but can you tell me the quickest way to Northwich?'

From the reaction of one small boy visiting Arley it would seem that stately homes are still regarded as the repository for all known vice and corruption. Looking into the cash box as he passed through the entrance, the little fellow asked a guide, 'Do you have thousands of pounds in there?'

'No, I'm sorry to say,' she replied.

'That's good,' said the boy earnestly, ''cos if you did, Robin Hood would come and take it off you!'

Noel Miller, the Duke of Northumberland's chauffeur, always pined after a uniform. When driving His Grace to official state functions, he would invariably bring up the subject, and press his employer to buy him a new outfit. On one occasion, he became particularly insistent on the point, adding that the suit he was wearing had been bought at a jumble sale.

The Duke's reaction was not quite what the driver had been expecting. 'Was it really? I must say it looks jolly smart! Would you get one for me next time you visit one of these sales?'

Breamore, in Hampshire, was lucky enough to gain a marvellous new guide some years ago, when their local policeman retired from the force. He was a larger than life character – handsome and broad shouldered with waves of thick, white hair. He stood totally erect, as ex-policemen usually stand, and had a devoted, little wife who only just came up to his waist. Despite this, they were a very close couple.

He had his own unique way of describing things; he also had a very broad Hampshire accent. On approaching a pair of Brussels tapestries by David Teniers, he would always say, 'Now we come to the Teneers tapestries.' On hearing this, a small boy once asked his mother, 'Cor Ma, did they really take ten years to make?' They are still known as the ten-year tapestries.

An early cricketing painting was characterized thus: 'This is "The Boy with the Bat", bat over his shoulder, two stumps in his left hand, ball's in his pocket.'

Whilst a fine display of 'The Guelphic Order' with framed letter in the Prince Regent's own hand, presenting the order to Field Marshal Sir Samuel Hulse, brought forth: ''Ere we have the Chain, Star and Ribbon of the Royal Hanoverian Order with letter from the King, wishing 'im all the best.'

The strong regional pronunciation, which he retained throughout his life, often produced even stranger effects. Introducing a painting of the Holy Family in a landscape he would say: ''Ere we 'ave Joseph and Mary with Charleybrest' (child at breast). Many of the visitors must have left the house theologically confused, to say the least.

The Devonshires at Chatsworth House used to have their own brewery, located in the stables. The beer was twice monthly pumped down a 400-yard, 3-inch lead pipe to the beer cellar in the house. This cellar contained twelve 100-gallon oak barrels – known as the twelve apostles – some of which still survive, complete with the family crest. At the time that the brewery was in operation Chatsworth employed over sixty gardeners.

In the 1950s the lead pipe was being salvaged for its scrap value to help meet the death duties on the estate of the late Duke. When the engineers reached the stretch of pipe running past the gardeners' mess they discovered a tap, which had evidently been used to divert the flow of ale.

Then it all began to make sense. No wonder such an unholy din had been heard coming from the quarters of the gardening fraternity, every time a quota of beer was piped across to the house! And no wonder that every second week – for one morning only – there was a mysterious decline in the standards of horticulture at Chatsworth.

The ring leaders were rounded up – all sixty of them – and given a sharp reprimand. Witnesses to the haranguing say that most of them seemed less contrite than concerned about the ebb in their ethanol supply. An understandable position to take, I would say.

The relationship between a butler and his employer has often been described as telepathic. Role reversal is frequent and spontaneous; misunderstandings rare indeed. Occasionally though, a combination of extreme apathy on the part of the servant, and burgeoning senility on the part of the master, can result in *communication breakdown*.

Patrick Lichfield relates a story told to him by Hugh Cholmondeley of an incident he witnessed as a small boy whilst staying at Tatton Park. He had been invited for dinner by the bountiful Lord Egerton, whose many endearing qualities included a ready ability to misinterpret completely what was being said to him.

He was also punctual to a fault. Thus it was that, at eight o'clock precisely, the host marched himself and his guests into dinner before the butler had had time to announce it. Visibly ruffled, the exacting peer sat down at the head of the table, arms crossed in the manner of a child refused candy, and waited for the food. Nevertheless, by the time the hapless butler had engineered the pouring of the wine, the Lord was in deep conversation with his neighbour. He had evidently forgotten the delay.

Still, his retainer felt bounden to apologize for his sloppiness and, scarlet-faced, he approached, offering the following explanation: 'I'm terribly sorry about the lateness of dinner this evening, my Lord, but you see the chef has been having a dreadful struggle with the Aga.'

Lord Egerton looked slightly perplexed by this revelation. He was silent for a few moments, then appeared to make a mental connection of startling implications: 'The Aga! Good God, I didn't even know the chap was in the country!' He pondered the puzzle briefly, dismissed it with a shrug, and tucked into the smoked salmon pâté.

The butler shuffled back to the kitchens, an affectionate smile playing across his lips.

Codes and passwords are essential in maintaining the steady and seamless flow of information between a butler and his employer. Lady Dorothy Meynell of Hoar Cross Hall (now a prestigious health farm) in Staffordshire frequently made use of this system whilst entertaining in the dining room.

Owing to an unfortunate tendency on the part of her nose to form a drip during dinner, she had instructed the butler to advise her of any accumulating moisture with the words, 'Roger's at the door, M'lady.' The guests would invariably take this to mean that some footman or other had returned from an errand, and had some news to deliver. The hostess would then excuse herself and make for the powder room.

But the arrangement was by no means infallible. A compulsive story-teller, Lady Meynell often had to be warned of Roger's proximity several times before appropriate action was taken. On one famous occasion, she was in the midst of a more than usually salacious tale about a favourite cousin, when the drop swelled and began to shimmer dangerously at the tip of her nose. The butler, who had been monitoring the progress of the globule through the first course, felt now was the time to step in. Coughing politely, he said, 'M'lady, Roger's at the door.' The warning had no effect whatsoever as the hostess ploughed on with her scandalous story.

So the butler issued a second, sterner warning: 'Roger's at the door, M'lady!'

Still no reaction from the rambling hostess, who was coming to the eighth consecutive climax of her recital.

Finally, in stentorian and admonitory tones, the assembled company was informed: 'Roger's in the soup, M'lady!' – and indeed he was.

The Marquess of Cholmondeley, of Houghton Hall near Kings Lynn, and Cholmondeley Castle in Cheshire, remembers a tale involving a less than diplomatic butler.

When my father first moved to Cholmondeley, he inherited an ancient retainer who had served under his grandmother. Once the butler appeared whilst my father was enjoying a short snooze to say that a certain gentleman was on the phone.

'Oh blast,' yawned my father, 'you'd better tell him I'm out.'

The butler doddered off, and my father heard him pick up the receiver in the hallway, and say, 'Sorry, but 'is Lordship says 'e's out.'

Ivor Spencer has been one of Britain's top toastmasters for many years. He was also toastmaster at my wedding, which is how I know him. The job looks easy to an untrained eye, but in fact requires mental agility, a very detailed knowledge of etiquette and an unflappable disposition.

The Ivor Spencer International School for Butler Assistants (trained British style) was founded some years ago, an institution that is famed worldwide for the quality of its training, and the skill of its graduates.

It is for this reason, as well as many others (not least his splendid sense of humour), that I approached him prior to the writing of this book, and asked whether he might know of any amusing anecdotes involving butlers and their employers. Ivor was cagey. It wasn't that he didn't know any but rather that, as he explained to me, the nature of his work requires, above all, *discretion* ... Mentioning names is forbidden in the butler's bible, and with good reason – an essential rule of buttling demands that the practitioner must, at appropriate times, be struck deaf, dumb and selectively blind. The idea of selling stories about your employer to a national tabloid would appal any well trained butler, he said.

Thankfully I am not a national tabloid, nor do I offer money for tittle-tattle (however scandalous). What I am is an old pal of Ivor's. Because of this we have the following stories, for which the toastmaster *extraordinaire* will be rewarded in heaven, if not on earth. (Names withheld for reasons outlined above.)

The first story concerns our 'cousins' abroad. For many Americans, a butler is the ultimate status symbol; more exclusive than a Mercedes, and less dangerous than a helicopter, the British servant spells wealth and class in large capital letters. Ownership means that you have scaled the social pinnacle, and are now taking a protracted winter holiday on its select slopes. But like many things in the United States, one is rarely enough.

A butler of Ivor's was once placed by an agency with a family in Oklahoma. As part of his duties he had to answer the telephone, and this he did in the manner he'd been taught: 'The Lee (fictitious name) residence, Jennings the butler speaking, may I help you?'

The Lees were less than happy with this, and instructed him to say in future, 'The Lee residence, Jennings the assistant butler speaking, may I help you?'

Poor old Jennings was understandably confused, and a little hurt by this demotion, for as far as he knew, he was working completely alone ...

Ivor is often booked by top hotels to act as toastmaster at weddings, but this means that he usually doesn't meet any of the bridal party in advance. On one particular occasion he had been booked by the Savoy, and the first he saw of the guests was when they arrived from the chapel.

The bride came into the hotel first with an extremely smart but elderly gentleman on her arm. The old coot staggered up to Ivor and asked him: 'Where do we stand to receive the guests?'

Ivor pointed out the position near a resplendent arrangement of flowers, adding 'Though, sir, it is not necessary for you to receive them as grandfather of the bride.'

The gentleman drew himself up to his full height, and fumed: 'For your information, I am the bridegroom.'

The toastmaster got an earful, and between the snarls understood that the bride had been the octogenarian's secretary, but was now marrying him, as was her privilege, thank you very much, and how dare you presume to …

Ivor has learned not to judge a book by its cover, however dilapidated it may be.

He once acted as master of ceremonies at a very grand party in Mayfair, probably the smartest and certainly the most expensive area of London. The event was put on by a well-known Duchess and festivities continued through the night until four o'clock in the morning, when the hostess took up position in the front doorway to say 'Goodbye' to the stragglers.

During the party she had given strict instructions to her butler that Ivor Spencer and the members of the band performing at the dance should be given nothing other than the finest food and drink. They should be treated as honoured guests.

Naturally, not wanting to be churlish in the face of such marked generosity, the band had taken full advantage of the offer – though Ivor, a lifelong teetotaller, stuck to his accustomed orange juice – and between them, consumed a fair few magnums of the finest Dom Pérignon champagne. The band leader had put away so much in fact that, in a fit of audacity, he conspired to smuggle out an extra magnum which would go down very well, he said, with some scrambled eggs at home. He made for the exit, the bottle cunningly hidden beneath the folds of his overcoat.

He was evidently not a practised shoplifter; for when he paused at the door to say farewell to the magnanimous Duchess, the champagne bottle slipped from his grasp, slid rapidly down his trouser leg, and exploded into glittering crystals on the stone floor. The band leader could only watch in horror as the prized liquid lapped the shoes of the Duchess, and trickled out of the porch on to the steps below.

He prepared himself for a night in the cells.

But he had not reckoned on the cool munificence of his employer. She looked at the shattered glass, then at the musician, and calmly turned to her butler: 'James, would you please bring another bottle of Dom Pérignon for this gentleman. He seems to have dropped his.'

The butler strode off in the direction of the kitchens, whilst the musical virtuoso struggled to find the right words. There was no need. Stepping agilely from the pool of champagne, the Duchess took him by the arm and began thanking him in the most profuse terms for an exceptional evening.

When the magnum appeared, she took it from the butler, placed it in the hands of the confounded band leader, and let him pass into the night. But not before offering a most unusual apology: 'I'm so sorry about your new bottle of champagne! I notice it isn't properly chilled. Do forgive me!'

Another time Ivor was working at the Dorchester Hotel on an important lunch, when a Cabinet minister called him over to the top table.

'Ivor', he said, 'could you possibly help me out here? I seem to have lost my false teeth.'

Ivor was somewhat taken aback by this startling admission, but could see all too clearly that the minister was indeed *sans* dentures. The august politician went on to explain the root of his dental dilemma. In meticulous detail, he advised the toastmaster of the situation, as though he were addressing the House on a particularly grave matter. 'You see the problem we have here, Ivor, is one of trying to run before you can walk! When fitted with a new set of teeth, one naturally assumes that the things will stay put. But one is wrong, terribly wrong, as the present state of affairs will testify …'

Ivor listened intently as the story of the missing gnashers unfolded. The minister had been to the dentist that morning, where he was equipped with a fresh pair of false teeth. At lunch, he had started to eat the roast lamb, but found to his dismay that the meat got stuck between the gaps. So he'd placed a napkin over his jaw, and began a surreptitious pruning of the obstinate fibres. In his struggles he'd succeeded in removing not only the unwanted lamb, but all the teeth as well, which had come unstuck at a crucial moment in his oral endeavours. Lowering the package from his mouth, he had left the loaded napkin on the floor next to his chair, hoping to find a moment to slink off to the men's room where he could rectify the problem. But just at that moment a waiter passed by, and seeing the soiled serviette on the ground, swooped down and whisked it away, contents and all, to the dirty linen basket, no doubt. The minister was concerned that there mightn't be much time before his teeth were swiming around in an industrial sized washing machine at the local laundromat. He had approached Ivor because he knew him to be the kind of man one could trust with such a delicate government mission.

The explanation over, Ivor rushed into the kitchens. He saw the little parcel sitting on top of a pile of linen. Discarding the used napkin and picking out a fresh one, he wrapped up the teeth and set off towards the top table again.

In this short interval the statesman had managed to get himself into some difficulties with another guest who had asked him a simple question. Without his molars and incisors, the minister felt powerless to do anything other than smile inanely back at her. By the time Ivor returned, he was in a state of high anxiety.

With the utmost secrecy, the toastmaster placed the bundle of cloth on the minister's lap, and with a polite cough, receded into the background.

It was thus that the man of affairs reclaimed his teeth, and his repartee, and now whenever the two men meet at a function they always follow the same script. 'What's on the menu today, Ivor?'

The toastmaster will always reply, regardless of the truth, 'Well, it's roast lamb of course, Minister!'

When the present curator – a lady – told her great-aunt of her recent appointment to this position at Woburn Abbey, the great-aunt telephoned another great-aunt and told her the good news. On being asked what the great-niece's duties entailed, the first great-aunt explained, 'I think she takes the collection, dear.'

One visitor we will never forget at Weston is the butler loaned to us by a typically wicked Japanese television company – the sort that makes those comedy endurance programmes. Suffering, cruelty and pain are, it seems, integral to the format – if you've ever seen a group of Japanese competitors being dragged along a stretch of gravel by a large tractor, wearing only their underpants, and the hilarity this occasions in the show's presenters, then you'll know the sort of thing I mean. If you haven't, then I suggest you watch Clive James.

We were contacted by Enterprise Aki, a production house in London, who had arranged for some poor chap to be imported from Japan, sent for a day's instruction at a top butler's school, then farmed out to a stately home where he might test his new skills. The purpose of the exercise, so they said, was to film the 'butler' as he went about his duties, and to make the experience as unpleasant and as humiliating for him as possible. For instance, they wanted to drop him off at the nearest rail or bus station to Weston, leave him there, and watch as he walked the rest of the way in his heavy butler's uniform. I pointed out the unfairness of the scheme, saying this would involve a hike of at least three miles. The producer was delighted.

Very soon after the arrival of the butler, I realized that we too had been selected for satirical abuse. I learned from a series of investigations that the star of the show was in fact a well-known Japanese comedian, and that the producers meant to ridicule us quite as much as they did him.

This seemed an especially dastardly way of going about things; not content to stitch up one of their own, they wanted to lampoon everyone else involved, even those who had agreed to help them. My suspicions were first aroused when the butler brought us breakfast in bed. I knew that he was to be filmed ironing a copy of *The Times* in the downstairs pantry, preparing the breakfast, then serving it to us in our bedroom.

He entered the room as planned, and after hovering by the bedside for a while, proffered a cup to my wife. She was just about to take it, when the butler suddenly snatched his hand away, and in a most peculiar manner began slurping the drink himself. Now I know for a fact that 'checking for poisoned tea' no longer features in the syllabus of butler training courses. From the titters behind the lenses, I quickly understood that our stunned expressions were going down very well, and that the scene would, no doubt, make excellent television for a rapturous Japanese audience. So I let the comedian get on with his performance unimpeded, and resolved to put a spanner in the works at a later date.

An opportunity presented itself when I was down by the park pool, a lake about half a mile from the house. The camera crew, for some reason best known to themselves, wanted to film the butler running across the fields in his tails and striped trousers as though on an urgent errand.

I espied the squat, tubby figure of the Japanese butler as he came bumbling through the park towards me. The strange thing was that he was holding his shoes above his head, which gave him the look of a soldier on military punishment. The producer was doubtless responsible. I became uneasy, and sensed that a practical joke was about to be played. The feeling was compounded by the manner of the comedian when he eventually arrived. Catching his breath, and mopping the sweat from his forehead, he eyed me nervously: 'Terephone call for you, my Rord!'

'Who is it, then?' I asked suspiciously.

'Solly?'

'Who is it on the telephone?' I queried for a second time.

'Er ... er ... don't know, my Rord,' he stammered, looking distinctly worried, as though he knew the game was up.

'Well I can't take a telephone call from just anyone,' I lied. 'So go back and find out who it is.'

The butler looked devastated. Muttering a cursory 'Light, my Rord', he trundled wearily back to the house and disappeared into the middle distance. Round 2 to me!

Maybe it was their lack of success with the phoney telephone call plan. Or maybe spite against a comedian who had failed to perform his role convincingly, but from that point on, the television company decided to leave me alone, and concentrate their energies on the original target.

They had bought a cheap Chinese vase, which looked somewhat similar to the antique ones we have at Weston. They then arranged for my house manager, Steve, to hand it to the unfortunate butler in such a way as to force an accident. When the accident duly occurred and the top of the vase went crashing to the floor, the man's expression progressed from one of abject horror to complete mortification. He stared at the broken remains of what he imagined to be a priceless family heirloom, and just when I thought he was going to commit spontaneous hara-kiri, I stepped in to assure him that it was just a mistake and that he shouldn't blame himself. This sort of thing has them rolling in the aisles in Japan, as it does here ...

But in Japan they evidently like to hammer the point home. The next day they asked me to present the unbroken bottom half of the vase to the star as a leaving present. He was genuinely overwhelmed by this act of generosity, little realizing that he was now the proud possessor of a strikingly average piece of modern ceramics, not a Ming relic, or anything like one. The cruelties of Japanese comedy are manifold.

I never saw the finished programme. In the months following the butler's visit, whenever I telephoned the office of Enterprise Aki, I always got a dead tone. Maybe they went bust and the show was cancelled; it's not entirely unlikely. But something that happened to me at Weston that same year makes me think otherwise.

We were holding a dinner for Jaguar Cars, and I spotted three representatives of the Japanese distributorship coming in through the front hall. They seemed to be in a state of high amusement. As I approached, one of them pointed at me and burst out: 'Aha! Rord! Yu velly funny!' the other two collapsed into a fit of hysterics, and clutching their sides, joined in, 'The Rord! Velly funny!' I took this in my stride, and began laughing myself, lest I should appear distant and humourless. I never found out what the joke was. But I have the distinct impression that it might have been me, and that Enterprise Aki did a pretty good job of sending me up after all.

The mythology surrounding butlers, which caricatures them as incompetent and befuddled geriatrics whose only real purpose lies in getting drunk at their employer's expense, is pretty unfair. Over the ages, stately home retainers have been known to form intimate relationships with the bottle ... but to suggest that they were too addled to camouflage their activities is a gross distortion. In many cases, head butlers have managed to polish off a household's entire supply, single-handed and without detection. Whether this had more to do with the cluelessness of the master than the cunning of the servant is, however, not for us to say.

Many years ago we had a butler at Weston Park, who rejoiced in the wonderful name of Wolf, pronounced 'Woof', like a dog's bark. A perfect example of the silent, efficient retainer – never intruding but always on hand in a crisis – he excelled at his craft, even though he was often a little unsteady on his feet.

One day my grandfather was holding a summer lunch party, and the butler was pouring out the white wine to accompany the meal, when one of the guests peered into the bottom of his glass and remarked: 'Quite extraordinary ... this wine tastes just like cider!'

Many of the other guests who had also smelt a rat but, in the tradition of English tact, had kept quiet about it, now felt obliged to support the gentleman. A chorus of disapproval swept the lawn, in which it was agreed that the colourless liquid did indeed taste suspiciously of apples.

My grandfather, as perplexed as anyone at the discovery, was exceedingly embarrassed. Not wanting to be unfairly labelled as the kind of host who tries to pass off cider as vintage wine, he launched an immediate investigation.

The results were conclusive – it transpired that Wolf had, over a period of years, syphoned off half the white wine in the cellar, drunk it, and filled the empty bottles with a particularly cheap and obnoxious cider. On the day of the summer luncheon, he had obviously got confused and served one of the 'renegade' bottles by mistake.

This little slip was enough to save what remained of a much

depleted cellar. The butler was not charged for what he had consumed but, in the spirit of the times, told to consider it as severance pay.

When The Hon. Gerald Maitland-Carew (known to his friends as 'Bunny') was a child, the family lived in Southern Ireland. Their home was Castletown, which has often been described as the finest Palladian house in Ireland.

In 1957 they were celebrating New Year's Eve, when by tradition, the British Ambassador to Dublin always came to dinner with them. At that time he was a delightful but rather elderly gentleman called Sir Alexander Clutterbuck.

On this particular evening the butler, Murphy, who had been a servant in the house since 1914, had consumed rather too much New Year spirit. He was going through the conventional process of opening the drawing room doors to announce the arrival of Sir Alexander and his wife. Flinging the doors wide open, he proudly proclaimed: 'My Lord! The British Ambassador to Ireland, Sir Alexander Clutter and Lady Buck!', and hurriedly withdrew.

Another tale of wilful misappropriation comes from a certain stately home whose name we prefer not to mention, for reasons which will become apparent.

A celebrated wine auctioneer, with acknowledged expertise in the naming and dating of vintage port, was once invited for the weekend to this particular historic house. He accepted the invitation immediately, knowing that the owner kept an especially fine cellar, which the auctioneer meant to sample.

Unbeknown to him, the host and his family were

somewhat sceptical of their guest's talents and wanted to find out whether his skill was genuine, or merely an elaborate confidence trick. They thought long and hard, and eventually came up with a scheme which would settle the matter once and for all, or so they hoped.

A few hours prior to the connoisseur's arrival, a member of the family went down to the local pub and asked for a bottle of ordinary house port. This was drawn from the wood, transferred to a crystal decanter, then placed on the table to be drunk at the end of dinner.

During the meal, the host noticed with pleasure that his knowledgeable guest was behaving to form. At the presentation of each wine, the expert's demeanour would suddenly change from one of relaxed cordiality to pious introspection. His eyes would glaze over, and he'd begin what sounded like a monastic dirge on the quality of the drink in his hand, as he tossed and rolled the liquid round his glass. Finally he'd taste it, only to let forth a sigh of such sustained agony that one felt he might collapse at any moment.

After the pudding plates had been cleared away, the port was passed along the table in the usual way. The auctioneer followed its progress with the careful eye of the predator until at length the decanter was before him. He started up on his well-practised ritual of glass fondling, accompanied by a largely inaudible commentary, when the voice of the host boomed down the table: 'So, what do you make of the port then?'

'Quite superb,' came the assured reply. 'The year must be 1947, and the shipper can only be Taylor's.'

The whole assembly, who were all in on the joke, dissolved into fits of laughter. The unfortunate guest looked up, and feeling slighted by the incredulity surrounding him, held up a clenched fist in defiance. 'I tell you, the year is 1947, and the shipper is Taylor's! It is inconceivable that I am mistaken!'

His host, thinking the jape had probably gone far enough, felt it was time to own up to the familial plot. He sheepishly explained the trip to the pub, and the fact that the port couldn't possibly be anything other than a rather standard, modern one.

The auctioneer reddened, shook his head violently in exasperation, and left very early the next morning, believing his reputation to have been cruelly maligned.

The eldest son, though, was puzzled by the whole incident. So he decided to investigate, and slipped out of the house down to the local pub. He asked the landlord to show him where the port had come from.

'Well,' said the publican, as they trudged through the cellar together, 'the port was sold to the pub before my time, so I don't know who brought it in. But I do know that it came in these bottles, before it was poured into the cask.' He pointed out a row of dark bottles resting on a dusty shelf in the far corner of the cellar. 'I've never looked at them myself, but you're quite welcome to, if it interests you.'

'It most certainly does,' said the visitor, and stretched to pull one down.

Wiping the bottle clean, he uncovered a tattered label on which was printed: Taylor's 1947.

'My God, he was right after all!' he spluttered. And as if a single shocking revelation wasn't enough for one day, he instantly exclaimed, 'But this is my family's port! Who did you say sold it to you?'

His bewildered companion repeated that he had no idea, as it had been bought by the previous landlord.

After subsequent inquiries in the area, the mysterious hustler was discovered to be none other than the family's own trusted butler. He had been raiding the stately cellar for many years and selling the contents at a knock-down price to local innkeepers.

It is not known how the auctioneer reacted to this news

when it was relayed to him. But it can be assumed that, with his reputation restored, he permitted himself a smile at the family's expense. (Names not mentioned to avoid embarrassment)

Somerley, in Hampshire – designed by Samuel Wyatt in the mid 1700s – is renowned for the elegance of its interiors and its magnificent setting on the edge of the New Forest. The Earl of Normanton describes a tragic episode which took place at his ancestral home several years ago. He had recruited an Irish butler – ex-Irish Guards, with a typically Gaelic sense of humour – but we are pleased to record that, in this case at any rate, there were no suspicions of cellar abuse.

One weekend a guest arrived, brandishing a puppy which she had just bought. The little ball of fur didn't look too good on arrival, but as there is a strict rule of 'No dogs in the bedrooms' at Somerley (for fear of irreparable damage to curtains and fabrics), it had to be put downstairs for the night in a room with a stone floor.

During the night the puppy sadly passed away, and was discovered by the butler early the next morning. He put the poor creature in a very smart 'Lobbs' shoe box, complete with sepulchral padding, and took this to the dog's owner. Gently breaking the news to her, he made a sweeping bow and, in his inimitable way, offered his services: 'Madam, would you like me to reverse my stiff collar and say a few prayers at your little one's funeral?'

The offer was politely declined, and the lady crept into the woods and buried her puppy in private.

Baffling idiosyncrasies are, of course, not restricted to male members of staff. In the interests of sexual equality, we feel obliged to relate the following tale of gastronomic invention, which comes from Thirlestane Castle in Berwickshire, Scotland.

Our source tells us that many years ago, the then chatelaine, Ivy, Countess of Lauderdale, had a cook called Nan, whose kitchen practice was very much her own. For instance, scones featured largely and disproportionately within her repertoire. So much so that if the eggs required for a house party's breakfast arrived an hour or two before schedule, they would be converted into soft cakes on the spot, and served with the rashers of bacon and the grilled mushrooms. This would very often leave the guests utterly mystified and marvelling at the innovations of Scottish cuisine.

On one celebrated occasion, a guest appeared with his Labrador shooting dog, and a couple of tins of Pedigree Chum. He presented the tins to Nan with a request that she prepare them for consumption after the shoot the next day.

At dinner that same evening, our informant saw the Countess flinch noticeably as she tucked in to the Brown Windsor soup. She made no comment, but from the fragile lumps of reconstituted meat floating in the bowl, it was quite obvious to what purpose the Pedigree Chum had been applied.

Following the soup incident, one of the party was especially keen to meet the culinary magician in the flesh. He was led into a vast subterranean kitchen, where he espied, through the steam, a stocky figure dressed in Wellingtons and a granny-print dress. Nan (for it was she), with her bottom rested on the cool hob of an ancient Esse, was stirring a cauldron which boiled furiously on the adjacent hot surface. She seemed impervious to the discomfort such a position would normally induce, and the guest began to wonder whether he was in the presence of a mystical guru. What would she do next? Levitate and fly round the ceiling?

He resisted the urge to flee, and watched nervously as the cook eyed him up and down. Finally, she spoke: 'But my, you've grown!'

Considering they'd never met, this was plainly a testament to her mastery of the paranormal, but the bemused visitor never did find out who she thought he was.

Harewood House near Leeds, home to the Earl of Harewood and family, is famed for its Robert Adam interiors, as well as its furniture which has been described as the richest collection of Chippendale in the world. Much of it was made especially for Harewood by Thomas Chippendale.

Being one of the eight treasure houses of England, Harewood House is, understandably, security sensitive. Many years ago, during a spate of bomb attack warnings and foiled attempts elsewhere, the owner and top staff got together to devise a test for their existing safety procedures.

The house opening manager, who had obviously been reading too many SAS manuals, wanted to construct a 'dummy' explosive, and secrete it behind a radiator in one of the rooms. The rest of the staff would then be given instructions, in view of the warnings, to make a particularly thorough search.

The plan was given the go-ahead, and the manager got to work. He assembled the charge out of a torch battery, some wires, a bit of plastic and an empty cigarette packet, and put it in place. The staff were then given their orders and the hunt began.

Three days later one of them stumbled accidentally upon the makeshift bomb. I believe it took rather less time for the owner to vent his feelings about the thoroughness of the search.

In view of this, the manager decided to try a different tack. He went down to the village telephone box, and placing a handkerchief over the mouthpiece, made a phone call to the receptionist in the front hall. 'I have a warning for you – there's a bomb in the house!' he hissed.

'I beg your pardon. Would you mind repeating that?'

'I said, there's a bomb in the house!'

'Is there? Oh, thank you very much,' came the somewhat inadequate reply, and the receptionist hung up.

The manager tore back to the house, fully expecting to find Harewood in the throes of a concentrated, seamlessly efficient investigation. Entering the front hall, he came upon the receptionist flicking through the pages of a glossy magazine.

Thunderstruck by this total lack of activity, the manager enquired: 'Didn't you have a telephone call a short while ago.'

'Oh yes, there was someone who kept on saying "There's a bomb in the house, there's a bomb in the house!" '

'Yes, and?' said the manager, unable to believe his ears.

'Oh well, he didn't leave his name I'm afraid, so I couldn't tell you who it was.'

The Earl would like me to tell you that all this is ancient history, and the present staff at Harewood are a by-word for alertness.

⚜

That's Entertainment

Food has always fascinated me. At school I made simple meals for my friends, such as scrambled eggs on toast. On my year off teaching in Ghana, self-catering came with the territory. The indigenous cuisine was of a sufficiently volatile nature to stimulate the most reluctant of chefs. When I finally returned to England, weighing in at just over eight stone, the men's department at Harrods demoted me to the boy's department, which pleased me no end. Sadly, it was only a matter of time before my new trousers failed to meet in the middle.

This had something to do with my culinary exploits at university, where I learned to produce three-course dinner parties using only two gas rings and a toaster – quite a logistical feat! (At Cambridge I also came to understand a valuable tenet of home entertaining – guests are far less likely to criticize your efforts with a bottle of good claret inside them.)

These early fumblings with food weren't exactly the perfect apprenticeship for my career as a restaurateur, but they helped point me towards that profession, which was to become a crucial part of our campaign to keep Weston financially viable.

The family were doing almost next to nothing in the way of catering in the main house at the time of my father's death in 1981. Shortly afterwards I realized why.

A local couple were going to be married at Weston, and had, optimistically, asked us to provide a sumptuous repast suitable for the occasion. The meal was a complete disaster. The sauce in the prawn cocktail slipped to the bottom of the glass, leaving the prawns pitifully exposed on top. The roast beef looked like chargrilled sledge-dog, tasted like Hush

121

Puppie, and proved highly efficient at liberating false teeth. Whilst the sherry trifle utterly belied its name, suggesting we had merely waved the cork from a bottle of British VP over a bowl of tinned fruit and jelly.

This was partly the fault of inexperienced local chefs, but it had more to do with a lack of foresight and coordination. If anyone is thinking of serving dinner to an agitated wedding party, they should remember this one golden rule: always work to a timetable well ahead of the actual hour. Reason: *The wedding photograph*. These are notoriously protracted affairs and on this occasion we underestimated by roughly half an hour: enough time to spoil the appearance and flavour of the food, rendering it virtually inedible.

Nothing can compensate for a ruined wedding; it's not as if you can hold it again the next week! The father of the bride had an apoplectic fit, blowing a gasket and several cylinder heads in the process. He was so incensed that at first he brushed aside offers of a generous refund – but later he came to his senses and grudgingly accepted a large reduction in the size of his bill. I made a resolution. The days of 'Carry on Catering' were over. From now on Weston was going to earn a reputation for professional service and mouth-watering food.

First we had to sort out the equipment. Up to the day of the wedding farce, we had been using shiny, plastic chairs; sturdy crockery and cutlery (the favoured implements of motorway service stations); and the kind of glasses readily acquired with a couple of tokens from participating garages; plus a selection of highly absorbent paper napkins. Not exactly Searcy's, you understand ... Unlike Searcy's though, we were reeling from the effects of an £8 million death duty bill – it is a desperately dismal but intrinsic feature of aristocratic life that dying is the most expensive venture you are ever likely to enter into.

Gradually we made the changes, squeezing money out of

each event to improve the next one. This was a constant struggle, but in time we had saved enough money to buy 120 decent banqueting chairs, appropriate Wedgwood crockery, together with Arthur Price classic silverware and to provide proper linen napkins (hired from the local laundry). The real revolution happened in the kitchens though. It's no good serving slops with silver. One of the first tasks was to widen our repertoire. There comes a time when it is no longer reasonable to expect this traditional Midlands menu to incite mass gastronomic frenzy:

Prawn Cocktail or Tomato Soup

Roast Beef with Yorkshire Pudding,
Vegetables, Gravy and Roast Potatoes

Trifle or Black Forest Gâteau

Tasty it may be, but I'm not sure it would have the Roux brothers reconsidering the direction of international cuisine. Most of all we wanted to make an impact – in fact, it was vital for the survival of Weston Park that we did.

So in 1982 we commenced what became known as Weston's Gourmet Dinners. This was, of course, a pretty silly name. We recognized that. None the less it seemed the easiest way to convey the quality of our cooking to an untrusting local clientele. (Shropshire people have not been noted for their tolerance of 'foreign, mucked-up stuff'. Many have been known to almost faint on first acquaintance with *Soupe de Poisson*.)

Before any local conversions could take place, however, we had to convince the press. Accordingly, an entire weekend was set aside in which we invited inspection from the media world with a chance for them to cast judgement on our progress.

The response both shocked and delighted us. A myriad of

journalists convened, including prominent food writers from the national papers and magazines. We had cast the die, and it had been thrown back at us. It was vital now for Weston's future that we were not found wanting.

The first night of the launch everything was going to plan. The dining room looked fantastic, thanks to the superior decorating powers of my mother. She had created an ambience that seemed to transport the act of eating from the functional to the exotic.

Worn out by an afternoon spent sweet-talking the press corps, it came as a relief to disappear into the kitchens and oversee the preparation of the food itself. I had asked my wife and the administrator at Weston Park to ensure that not all the guests sat down at the same time, as we were offering a small choice within each course. Things could get very complicated very quickly if we had to serve nearly one hundred champagne-fuelled journalists all at once.

Sadly, my wife, the administrator and the staff were powerless to prevent what happened next. I know nothing about the feeding habits of food critics and newspaper correspondents, but it would appear that they act instinctively and in unison, like a large herd of bison travelling at speed. Without any apparent signal, they can sweep the length of a drawing room and descend into an eating position within seconds. What started as a trickle developed into a stampede, and before I knew it, the whole crew were assembled fiddling expectantly with their napkins. Only a single venerable hack lingered, and he'd obviously fallen foul of the pre-dinner libations, as he appeared to be conducting a heated exchange with a curtain rail.

To make matters worse, the arsenal of toasters at our disposal decided now would be a good time to explode, fusing all the lights and ovens in the kitchen. Disorientated chefs fell over each other, cursing imaginatively, as they tried to engage the emergency system which consisted of two lamps and a collection of candles. Thankfully the candelabras and chandeliers in the dining room continued to function normally; only myself and a clutch of chaotic cooks knew of the black-out conditions within. I made a secret vow never to serve pâté again.

At last somebody found the right fuse, and we returned to a state of electricity.

From that moment, the dinner was an improbable but consummate success. Food flowed seamlessly from the kitchens; the guests ate, drank, and burped with gay abandon. Many of them, their faces gently glowing in the light of the chandelier, were gesticulating theatrically – a sure sign of an evening's success. I half expected someone to stand up and make an unintelligible speech.

During the meal I'd been rushing around like a man demented, stirring this, ladling that, and kicking the occasional toaster. My appearance could not be described as user-friendly; unsightly patches had formed in the expected places, and a spear of broccoli had somehow insinuated itself into my jacket pocket. So I changed hurriedly, taking a French shower – a quick squirt of aftershave in the more sensitive areas – and went out to chat to the diners. Some were past the stage of wholly rational comment, but the prevailing theme was one of congratulation, and a refusal to acknowledge the possibility of a power-surge in the pantry. After a while I stopped explaining the small delay before the first course; besides, I didn't want to confuse the guests any further.

That night I went to bed a happy man. The ensuing publicity for the dinner was lavish and generous in its praise: Gourmet Dinners were here to stay. The only problem now was how to domesticate a dozen malevolent toasters …

Some Salopians would rather gargle anti-freeze than sample international cuisine. Garlic has much the same effect on them as it does on Christopher Lee – momentary seizure followed by rapid flight. But prior to the first open Gourmet Dinner even I had no idea of the level of local hostility. It was extreme.

We had prepared, as part of a choice of main courses for the evening, Boned Leg of Lamb, filled with Garlic and Herbs, and served with a reduction of its Juices and Mushroom Stuffing. This was a classic French dish that had always proved most popular at my restaurant Bewick's in Walton Street. I expected it to sell prodigiously, but it proved anathema to the regional crew. They wouldn't touch it with a bargepole, let alone the knives and forks we had laid on.

Where had we gone wrong? Was it the stuffing, the juices, the time of year? Were there international 'lamb-friendly' days, this being one of them?

I decided to find out and approached what looked like a more or less communicable diner, casually inquiring: 'Not tempted by the lamb, sir?'

'Of course I'm not,' came the feisty reply as he pointed to the menu. 'It's got that blasted garlic in it!'

Pondering the logic of this, I confirmed the presence of a certain pungent root vegetable, but suggested that as it was part of the recipe, this was only natural.

'Natural, my foot!' came the swift reply. 'You don't cook lamb with garlic. And from the look of the other tables, I'm not the only one here who thinks so!'

This seemed to spell things out pretty clearly. But I was still troubled by the degree of community resistance. Perhaps the reason lay in the history of the area … I had heard tell that the Norman conquerors were particularly savage in their submission of the Black Country. Perhaps this had included the deployment of garlic as light artillery against the domestic population. Whatever the case, it didn't bode well for a series of Gourmet Dinners, if the district's dietary laws decreed the eating of anything vaguely foreign an indictable offence.

A few days later, my wife and I visited a local restaurant in Newport. We ordered a starter of garlic bread, which duly appeared – steaming, wholemeal loaves lightly sprinkled with fresh herbs. But after a few bites Joanne commented: 'Mmm … lovely garlic bread, but there appears to be something missing.'

'Strangely lacking in garlic,' I agreed. We called over the waitress and asked for an explanation.

'Yes, that's right, sir. There's no garlic – we used to have it, but too many customers complained, so we took it off, and put herbs on instead.'

Not wishing to start a stimulating discussion about the finer points of the Trade Descriptions Act, I let the matter pass. But in the car on the way home, I had an idea. If Shropshire restaurants were selling garlic bread under false pretences I could profitably reverse the equation.

So we created a new format for the next series of dinners, some three months later. Previously, the menu had included a selection of dishes within each course; from now on it was to be 'fixed'. At one of the gourmet evenings in this session, the following was presented: Boned Leg of Lamb, served with a reduction of its Juices and Mushroom Stuffing.

The recipe remained exactly the same as before, (in fact if anything we went heavy on the garlic); only the description was tampered with. But this proved enough to spur considerable numbers into booking for that particular weekend, including – I observed with pleasure – the voluble gentleman from a few weeks earlier.

Naturally, I sought his opinion at the end of the meal. 'I see you had the lamb this time, sir. I hope you enjoyed it.'

'Enjoyed it? It was bloody marvellous, sir! Even my wife remarked on the wonderful smell as it came to the table. Just as well you ditched that rotten garlic idea. No good would have come of it. May we have the recipe? We'd love to cook it at home.'

Thanking him for his kind words, with the delicate reminder that our recipes were ours and ours only, I strolled back to the kitchens; and, to my ears at least, the triumphant melody of the 'Marseillaise' accompanied me there.

We serve food to all sorts of customers. Most are delightful, and many return year after year. Some, as you know, are confirmed xenophobes; certain others see the dining experience as only vaguely linked to the consumption of food, and defying their digestive systems, plough through the fine wine as if it were tonic water. They tend to provoke meaningless altercations in the library after dinner, and polish off most of the brandy.

By far the most intriguing bunch I have nicknamed 'The 4 × 100-metre Sprint Squad'. They treat the meal like an Olympic relay race, something to be completed as quickly as possible lest the medals escape them. Quite what the point is, I have no idea. Perhaps they all convene at a later stage for an elaborate ceremony. 'Mrs Daniels representing Derbyshire collects the gold medal for fastest consumption of a Summer Pudding.'

One speedster in particular found fault with a special lunch we had organized for him. He wrote an exceptionally astringent letter, in which he declared that the meal had taken far too long and that he would not be using us again. Any serious complaint like that has to be investigated properly, but I quickly discovered that we had actually succeeded in serving his 120 guests a five-course lunch in under an hour and a half. Any faster than that and we would have had to equip the waitresses with roller skates.

Another tendency of certain British diners is to adopt the 'Whichever way you do it, we know better' attitude. This syndrome encompasses both sustained cynicism – the guest is on a mission to complain – and a joy in the art of 'back-seat cookery'. The slightest mishap will occasion a barrage of told you so's – enough to ruffle the feathers of the most tolerant maître d'hôte.

Nine times out of ten the complainants are mistaken anyway, but empirical truth does not sit well with the ostensible challenge: 'I must find fault with the food at least five times, otherwise the evening will have been a total failure.' Needless to say, the challenge is rarely too much for them – this bunch could go on all night, and frequently do.

I once got an extraordinary letter from a lady who took me to task on various aspects of her meal. Searching for her name among the reservations, I found that she wasn't even booked but had in fact enjoyed a dinner at another customer's expense. He and his wife had treated a private party of friends and relations to a veritable banquet in the small salon, where they'd received the most exacting service all night.

So slipping into detective mode, I got on the telephone and gently inquired of the beneficent gentleman whether he and his guests had been satisfied with their evening. 'Absolutely fine,' he said. 'Excellent food, good service, we all had a fabulous time. See you at the next series!'

In a more devilish mood, I might have pointed out that one of his guests had been less than impressed with the extent of his generosity. But I wanted to deal with that churlish individual myself.

The greater part of her letter had been devoted to criticism of the food. She complained that our menu planning was 'somewhat askew. Why, for instance, did you serve two pâtés as a starter?'

After two paragraphs of systematic nit-picking, she got on to the state of the pudding, 'Your Pavlova bases were "too" perfect. They must have been "bought in". I really think that if you advertise homemade food you should serve it!'

There's only one way to deal with ill-informed pedantry, and that's to turn the criticism round full circle. I therefore took considerable trouble in penning a letter which corrected the lady in painstaking detail on a number of points. Referring to the 'two pâtés' accusation, I explained that we had most definitely served only one, a Smoked Salmon Pâté – in the style of a mousse, wrapped in smoked salmon and accompanied by *sauce verte*. What she had mistaken for the other was in fact a rather special Game Terrine with a Cumberland Sauce. I offered to recommend a selection of excellent cookbooks that would adequately explain the difference.

After dealing with some minor points – such as the vegetables being undercooked, which 'didn't even have any sauce on' (how shocking!) – I came to the Pavlova plaint, the intent of which I deliberately misconstrued.

'Madam, what a delightful compliment you pay us when you consider our meringue bases to be "too perfect". They were of course homemade, as is all our food.'

We have welcomed the generous gentleman and his friends to Weston's Gourmet Dinners many times since. But one member of the party has been conspicuous by her absence. She must still be wondering about the content and quality of my apology.

Another regular visitor to our Gourmet Dinners suffered from a curious misunderstanding about the exact temperature at which to serve red wine.

(We store all our wines in the old Muniment Room, where the family documents used to be kept, which holds all the reds perfectly at the correct degree of warmth. When wine experts of old prescribed the precise temperature for clarets or burgundies as 'room temperature', they were of course dealing with pre-centrally heated houses, which tended to be a great deal colder than we are used to today. Red wine should be served neither chilled, nor warm, but somewhere in between. The modern tendency to place a bottle on the radiator to give it a quick blast is not only misguided, but damaging to the wine as well.)

Whenever we brought out a red for this particular gentleman, he would invariably send it back, saying it was 'far too cold'. After a series of emphatic rebuttals, by which time the staff were getting a little hot under the collar, we resolved to take the diner at his word and submerged the bottle in a pan of freshly boiling water, leaving it there for a full five minutes. We delivered the steaming bottle of Château Talbot to the table.

The response was unequivocal: 'You know this is the only dining establishment I've come across that knows the right way to serve red wine.'

As in most things, the customer is always right, even when he's actually wrong. Despite the fact that the gentleman was drinking the equivalent of mulled red wine, nearer to 'fever' than 'room' temperature, we appreciated the compliment.

At Constable Burton Hall, a lovely Palladian mansion in Yorkshire, Charles and Maggie Wyvill specialize in putting up house parties that are visiting the Yorkshire area. The guests usually spend the day outside, taking in the finer aspects and history of one of the most beautiful parts of the country, before returning for a relaxing, though sumptuous, dinner. Excellent food and wine is invariably laid on. As Charles and Maggie host every evening themselves, one has to admire their fortitude in retaining their figures.

New parties often need to be put at their ease. Even with a family and house as friendly as the Wyvills at Constable Burton, staying in a stately home for the first time can be an intimidating experience. So Charles developed a way of breaking the ice with people he didn't know.

At dinner Maggie would invite the guest on her right (normally, by custom the host of the party), to sip with her from a fine Elizabethan Loving Cup. At this point, Charles would feign jealousy, storm out of the room, only to return a few seconds later brandishing a shotgun. Pointing the weapon in the direction of the imbibing 'lovers', he'd empty both barrels down the table. This of course would elicit mass stupefaction, and much mopping of brows. But unbeknown to the guests, the shotgun had in fact been doctored with special shot-free cartridges, which whilst they put out a lot of noise and smoke, did no damage.

When the candles had been reignited, and the fumes had subsided, Charles would explain the little prank to a bewildered assembly, and could usually – though perhaps a touch unreasonably – expect the party to go with a swing thereafter. Terrifying experiences tend to encourage some sort of communication, after all.

Unfortunately, on one occasion, the Wyvills chose to perform the shotgun routine whilst Prince Bernhard of the Netherlands and various other royal personages were staying. As Charles let off the gun, twenty policemen and bodyguards burst into the dining room, formed a security circle round the table, and roughly disarmed what they took to be a paid assassin. Pistols at the ready, it took some time before they were willing to accept Charles's muffled protestations that it was all an elaborate trick designed to get the dinner conversation going.

After that particular débâcle, the Wyvills decided to lay the practical joke to rest. These days they favour more conventional welcoming techniques, though if you're lucky,

Maggie may still share the Loving Cup with you!

Among the many letters and contributions I received in the writing of this book, one stood out in particular.

—FAX TRANSMISSION –

To: Richard 'you can call me The Earl of' Bradford
From: Bob Payton, Pizza King, Baron of Beef, Prince of Pork

If all this seems deeply mysterious, perhaps I'd better explain that Bob Payton, who became the owner of Stapleford Park in Leicestershire, in 1987, was the man responsible for bringing the deep-pan pizza to the United Kingdom. He opened up the Chicago Pizza Pie Factory in London, and then consolidated his conquest of the market by introducing American ribs to a curious British public. The rest is history …

The Stapleford Park Hotel has been described as the best country house hotel in the world. Home to the Sherard family (who became the Earls of Harborough) for 450 years, this sixteenth-century house is now a mecca for those who appreciate both interior design and country sports. Bedrooms have been designed by no fewer than twenty arbiters of style and fashion, including Crabtree and Evelyn, Tiffany and Liberty's, and the only outdoor activity seemingly not on offer is big game hunting (Leicestershire has a shortage of leopards and rhino, I'm told). Anyway, over to Bob: 'One night at Stapleford Park, two reasonably well-spoken chaps came in for a drink. They looked like they'd already had a few, but I didn't pay much attention to them as they weren't causing any trouble. But as the evening wore on, one of the gentlemen began to get a little excitable. I went over to the duty manager and asked, "Who are these chaps then?"

' "Only a couple of publicans out for the night," he replied. This seemed perfectly credible in the circumstances, so I let the imbibers get on with their imbibing.

'After a while, I became curious. Returning to the duty manager, I inquired how he was so certain they were publicans. "Well, it's here in the book. They signed under 'The Marquess of Granby'. That's a pub, isn't it?"

'Well it might be; but on this particular occasion it was, in fact, the man himself – David Manners, son of the Duke of Rutland who lives at Belvoir Castle just ten minutes down the road.

'I should imagine that both he and his friend "suffered" proportionately the next morning.'

(Tragically Bob Payton died in a car accident in the middle of July 1994. Britain lost a great character who had revolutionized American-style restaurants in this country, and I lost a good friend.)

Status Quo and stately homes – an unlikely alliance, you think? Not if your name's David Cobbold, owner of Knebworth House in Hertfordshire, you don't.

Over the years Lord Cobbold and family have established their domain as the definitive rock festival venue in Europe. Famed for its championing of heavy metal – a musical form consisting largely of guitar solos played by men in spandex trousers – the annual Knebworth Weekend attracts thousands upon thousands of aurally challenged pilgrims each year. They gather at the height of summer, and depending on the climatic conditions, indulge in a variety of exotic sports. The cacophony acts as a catalyst – on wetter days, mud-fights are all the rage. When the weather is hot, a combination of herbal inhalation, mass nudity and sunstroke can produce scenes of apocalyptic proportions.

But it's not all sex, drugs and rock and roll. Events of this magnitude require careful planning; there are local organizations who need round-the-clock tranquillizing; concert promoters who must be monitored at every stage (it is not unheard of for members of the 'music biz' to get their sums catastrophically wrong); and the occasional performer whose instinct for self-advertisement has to be politely contained. Yet in all the glorious history of rock and roll at Knebworth, it is surprising how little blood has been shed. Human blood, that is ...

A few years back, a group by the name of Deep Purple – seminal to their fans, pretty impressive to anyone else – were coming to the end of their set. Seventy-five thousand leather-clad devotees roared with approval as the opening chords of the classic anthem 'Smoke on the Water' blasted out across a sea of mud and beer cans. They bellowed even louder when a fireworks display rivalling the best efforts of China's nuclear detonation team got under way. This was a party to remember, provided you were sober enough; and provided you weren't a bird of paradise ...

For, about two weeks later, a letter arrived at Knebworth from a firm of solicitors acting on behalf of a local parrot breeder.

The gist of the letter was that the general noise of the concert – and specifically of the fireworks – had alarmed the highly collectable parrots to such an extent that sixteen hatching eggs were broken, two parrots died and one broke its leg, representing a substantial loss to their clients. They were looking for compensation.

They found it, to the tune of a substantial settlement and to this day the Cobbolds make a point of liasing heavily with the local RSPCA. In the entertainment world zoological tragedy can strike at any time.

It is rare for the Girl Guides to get caught up in the action, but this is precisely what happened in 1976 when the Rolling Stones, arguably the most famous band of all time, came to play at Knebworth.

Their appearance had been memorably heralded some days before during the men's singles final at the Wimbledon Tennis.

Two men dressed as harlequins ran on to the Centre Court between sets. They bore a sign announcing: 'The Stones at Knebworth!' It was a masterpiece of publicity. It also caused acute embarrassment to a member of the Royal party, who witnessed the spectacle from the exclusive enclave of a Centre Court box. This was none other than David Cobbold's father, Lord Chamberlain at the time, who administered a proportionately turbulent dressing-down to his guiltless son when he got home later that evening.

The night before the concert was a particularly fine one so Mick Jagger and crew decided to run a spontaneous sound-check much to the delight of a tiny, but appreciative audience.

Unfortunately, someone had failed to mention the lingering presence of fifty Girl Guides who had permission to camp in the park till the end of the week. When the music began, the leader of the troupe, who had evidently been instructing her charges in the art of yodelling, stormed up to the house and broke into a last-minute meeting between David, the police and the promoter. Surprised by the apparition of a heavily perspiring middle-aged woman, whose dress sense bordered on the ridiculous, they gawped in silence as the leader began her lament: 'Would you mind telling me the meaning of that dreadful racket in the park? As you very well know, my girls and I are booked until Sunday evening, in which time we mean to practise a selection of traditional folk melodies. How do you expect us to sing, with that hideous noise going on?'

'Inaudibly, I hope,' thought David, but suggested instead that her girls might actually like to listen to a world-famous pop group, seeing they were so close at hand. This didn't go down at all well. 'They most certainly would not and I want it stopped at once!'

'Well then,' Lord Cobbold playfully countered, 'perhaps you'd like to tell the band to pipe down yourself.'

The bluff backfired; David could only watch in admiration as the stocky figure tore through the park, elbowed her way past security guards, and gaining access to the stage, grabbed Mick Jagger by the arm. History records the following exchange:

Guide Leader: 'Young man, I demand that you desist from this iniquitous commotion. I want you to lay down that instrument of torture and listen instead to my girls' stirring rendition of 'I Love to Go a-Wandering'. It might do you some good.'

Mick Jagger: 'O*!!* *!*, you old trout!'

A minor scuffle ensued, which ended badly for Mr Jagger. He was persuaded to leave the stage, and very soon the park echoed to a new kind of clamour.

Before the war, David's grandfather Lord Lytton, put up a sign:

> All ye who enter Knebworth Park
> One moment pause these words to mark.
> This property belongs to me
> As visitors here welcome be.

As you proceed please feel a duty
Not to disfigure Nature's beauty
With remnants of a picnic meal,
Silver paper or orange peel.
If you are smokers, be so kind
As not to leave a trail behind
Of cigarette cards, matches, rags,
Empty packets or paper bags.
If you have litter, leave it
In baskets furnished to receive it.
Give no cause to think you hateful
And I the owner will be grateful,
And ever gladly make you free
Of places that are loved by me.

This presented an irresistible temptation to one concert-goer, who graciously added the following lines:

Don't leave your roaches in the grass,
It's best to stash them in your . . . .,
Remember, all you doped buffoons,
The Lord won't take to coker's spoons
And if you feel the urge to mate,
To procreate, to copulate,
Just think not all will have your luck.
There'll be bad vibes if he sees you . . . .,
– get down and get with it!

Obviously a poet laureate in the making ...

As you have no doubt by now realized, we tend to host all kinds of events and parties. But when we received a booking from a Mrs Peggy Newfield of Atlanta, Georgia, who wanted to visit Weston with a class of graduating students from her School of Etiquette, because she wished to introduce her alumni to the beautiful houses and manners of the British aristocracy, we knew we were in for some fun.

Shortly afterwards I got a phone call from BBC Radio asking if there was anything going on at Weston in the near future that they might cover for their programme, *The Colour Supplement*. I suggested that an instructress of etiquette from the USA and her party of young girls might be of interest, and they agreed.

Mrs Newfield was ecstatic when I informed her, during our preliminary discussions, that the BBC wanted to record her school's overnight sojourn in the house. Not exactly a back runner in the publicity stakes, she leapt at the opportunity, and the meeting was set up.

The night of the visit arrived, and it became clear that the BBC reporter was keen to put on a lighthearted – rather than strictly documentary – piece of broadcasting. As the teenage girls descended for dinner, the theme from *Gone with the Wind* was used as background music, and he described the scene for the listeners with some relish: 'The beautiful young women glide down the staircase, their braces glistening in the lights of the chandeliers.'

This was a reference to the apparatus in their mouths, you understand, and it was apparent that some of the girls were barely out of nappies. (One of them rejoiced in the wonderful name of Tiffany Youngblood, and looked like a little Dresden doll with long flowing red hair.) The others were fifteen going on twenty-one, very precocious and undeniably glamorous. They all spoke with the most drawling Deep South accent, which can be quite intoxicating if you're not used to it.

We sat down to dinner. The table was positively festooned with flowers and silver candelabra, so much so that when Mrs Newfield took her position at one end, with myself at the other, we could barely see each other. As the eating began, I realized that, far from being their tutor, I was about to be given a short, sharp lesson in American manners. Politeness and delicacy in the Deep South dictate that you eat criss-cross, by which I mean you cut your meat up as normal with your knife in the right hand, put the knife down, then transfer the fork from your left to the now empty right hand, and eat the food with that – an extraordinarily fiddly process. I thought better of experimenting with it. Similarly bizarre was the manner in which they sat in between courses. I always tend to be rather slumped, with my elbows resting on the table. Mrs Newfield and her pupils sat much more demurely with their hands in their laps. I started to feel like a bit of a slob, but couldn't bring myself to copy the girls, as it struck me as an altogether artificial, not to say compromising position for a man to adopt.

After dinner, with the radio crew still recording, we retired to the library, and the reporter began to interview the headmistress. 'So, Mrs Newfield, how did you find Lord Bradford?'

'Lord Bradford?' she replied, basking in the attention. 'Lord Bradford was sitting twenty-five feet away from me at the other end of the room, with candles coming out of his ears!'

I appreciate that our dining room table is quite long, and that the decorations can tend to get in the way of a down-table conversation, but even so this seemed like a remarkably literal answer to a fairly straightforward question. Still, I wasn't prepared for her next bout of plain speaking.

When the reporter asked her about the hands-on-lap technique, she said, 'O yah. One time, when I was dining in France, the hostess turned to me and said, "Mrs Newfield, why are you sitting with your hands like that, are you playing with yourself?" '

I could see what the hostess had meant, and said, just

audibly, 'That's one of the reasons I always keep my hands well in view!' (The other, of course, is the long tradition of aristocratic apathy which teaches us to slouch at the dinner table, elbows out in front.)

Despite the fact that the Atlanta party seemed really rather uninterested in the rules of British etiquette, and much more keen to show us theirs, we were sorry to see them go, as the whole evening had been wonderfully spontaneous, and diverting.

But sadly, I don't think they'll make a return visit to Weston. A few of the girls had heard stories about ghosts haunting the corridors of ancient British houses, and had as a result got very little sleep during their one night with us.

Though Weston could not possibly be a friendlier place – and to my present knowledge there have never been sightings of doppelgängers, or rumblings of poltergeists at the house – the girls got so worked up they decided to crowd into adjoining bedrooms, with up to three in one bed, and left the next morning utterly exhausted. Perhaps if they had studied British etiquette a little more closely, they might have learned that one of the first requirements is a stiff upper lip, and could have avoided unnecessary fatigue.

About fifteen years ago, we held a rather smart dance in the house. At that time, we hadn't yet strengthened the cattle grid across the haha, linking the main drive with the front carriage ring of Weston Park so that it could take coaches. This meant that the passengers had to alight on the far side and march the last 100 yards to the house. They didn't actually have to traipse across the cattle grid, as there was a narrow pedestrian bridge at the side, decorated with round stone balls on the ground at either end. But they had to walk for their dinner none the less.

On less formal occasions and as long as it wasn't pouring down with rain, this presented no particular problem. However, on the night in question, we had organized an especially prestigious dinner dance, and many of the ladies came dressed in long, flowing ballgowns. These garments are fragile things at the best of times. They are decidedly unsuited to the delights of fell-walking, or white-water rafting, but have been known to survive the odd encounter with a concrete walkway. Sadly, this was not to be one of those moments.

A lady of pronounced sartorial distinction came to grief with one of the stone balls on the pedestrian bridge, and tore her dress slightly at the bottom. Normally this would elicit no more than a frown. On this occasion it brought on a torrent of cursing and wailing the like of which has not been seen since the day Rudolph Valentino died. By the time the woman had completed her walk across the carriage ring, she was in a right stew.

The staff, dodging verbal uppercuts, did their best to mollify her. They carried out a rough repair on the damaged dress, but this was evidently not enough to salvage the evening for the petulant damsel.

The following day she wrote an angry letter to the administrator, which tore him off a strip for not doing his job properly. She signed off with the final furious flourish, 'In future, would you kindly ensure that your balls are painted white, so that they can be clearly identified in the dark.'

Whilst we were keen to make amends, this action seemed a little drastic, even by our standards, so we reinforced the cattle-grid instead. The administrator, who hadn't fancied an afternoon of precious self-daubery, was much relieved.

The 11th Duke of Northumberland tells of a would-be thespian in his family

It was my Aunt Diana's (the Duchess of Sutherland) only part in a school play; just one line of dialogue, more of an exclamation than a sentence. She was to run on stage at a certain point, there'd be a pistol shot, and Diana had to look terribly surprised and say, 'Oh! A pistol shot!'

In the event even this proved too much for her. She scurried on at the precise moment, the pistol went off as directed, and she exclaimed, 'Oh! A postal shit!'

She tried, in vain, to remedy the verbal slip, 'Oh! A shistol pot!' ... 'Oh! An apostle shat!' and so on, until in the end I believe she got it right, having totally eliminated the element of surprise.

Sporting Chance

The running costs of Weston Park are enormous. After the death of my father, we were stretched to think of ways and means to keep it going. I soon realized that the odd party here and the occasional craft fair there wasn't likely to be enough. We had to be imaginative, and use the parkland at our disposal – over 900 acres of it – to maximum financial effect.

For several years we'd been putting on air displays in the park, thanks in part to the perennial generosity of the Royal Air Force who had in certain years even arranged for the Red Arrows to make a spectacular appearance. To begin with these had been a great success, bringing in the punters by the bus load.

But it soon became apparent that we would not be able to count on the cooperation of the RAF indefinitely. With more and more RAF stations putting on their own shows, resources were necessarily limited, and some years they simply couldn't help us out. Fortunately we had never had to rely on the RAF completely, and right from the first display we had been delighted to secure the services of a bunch of amiable, aerobatic maniacs. 'The Barnstormers Flying Circus', as they were called, were a group of individuals who spent the week in fairly mundane jobs, only to entrust their lives at the weekends to an assortment of dangerously delicate fighter planes for the entertainment of crowds.

They provided the main content of our event, and year after year stupefied the Weston audience with their mad-cap antics. Admittedly, some of the more dramatic stunts bordered on the disingenuous. A regular act, named 'Col. Crackshot', had one of the men riding atop a Tiger Moth, whilst shooting balloons off a board to which a young lady had been ceremoniously pinned. The balloons formed a circle around the girl, and every time the Colonel seemingly 'missed' one of his targets, the crowd issued a collective 'Ooooh', seriously believing that the bullets were real, and that they were just about to witness the first fly-past fatality in Weston's history.

Or so we liked to think anyway. I'm sure that most of the spectators realized that we hadn't actually employed a military lunatic to loose off revolver shots at an innocent female whilst balancing on an aircraft doing some 100 m.p.h. There are limits to what we'll do for money.

On the other hand ... one of the most successful and aesthetically pleasing stunts featured an attractive young lady flying around strapped to a small plane. We called this 'The Girl on the Wing', and each year milked it for as much publicity as we could. Before the days of political correctness, when such things were possible, we'd hold a beauty parade of nubile young locals, all of whom (or so we told the press anyway), had a lifetime ambition to ride a Tiger Moth. Why they'd want to do this, I couldn't imagine. But the news people lapped it up, which was the real purpose of the exercise, if the truth be told.

Publicity is a demanding mistress, though. Even more so is a stately home. The need to supply both can turn normally sane individuals into the most quixotic of optimists. I put the following chapter of incidents down to this irresistible condition, which can strike the owners of historic houses at any time.

Despite the success of 'Col. Crackshot' and 'The Girl on the Wing', we were increasingly pushed to come up with new ideas. The crowds were getting correspondingly smaller each year, threatening the viability of the annual air display. On years when the weather was poor, we made no profit at all and at times the future of Weston's air display looked uncertain. Drastic action was required, so I went to see the then administrator, Christine Lakeland, one morning with what I thought was the solution to our problems. I put it to her that instead of 'The Girl on the Wing' we might profitably enact 'The Earl on the Wing'. She looked at me incredulously, and said: 'But Lord Bradford, you know as well as I that you're the last person who should be going around strapping himself to aeroplanes.'

She was right; but not for the reasons you might expect. It wasn't that I was too stuffy to sit astride a Tiger Moth for the amusement of the Bank Holiday masses. Far from it ... The administrator was simply referring to an accident I had had in 1971 whilst touring Australia. I was left semi-paralysed for four months after a particularly nasty car crash, and spent a long time in hospital. Ever since then, I have suffered from perpetual back pain. Being tied to a fast-moving aircraft is probably not the best treatment for it. But I had no time for medical niceties. In my eyes it was either 'Earl on the Wing' or 'Earl on the Run from the Bank Manager', so we went ahead with the scheme.

As the press day approached I began to regret my impetuosity. It wasn't so much the prospect of severely damaging my back that worried me, more the implications of whirling around at 2,000 feet in a contraption designed for specifically internalized travel. But it was too late to back out now. The administrator, after her initial misgivings, was preparing for the event with an enthusiasm I could only regard as distinctly suspicious.

We got the highest turnout ever – two camera crews, five national press photographers, and a host of local reporters. Excitement was in the air. I couldn't help reflecting that I would soon be joining it.

The details of my stunt flight were explained to me in lurid detail. First, I was to be strapped on to a metal contraption on the top of the plane, then photographed at ground level.

Next, I would take off, sweep over the grounds a few times, allowing the press helicopter to get some aerial shots, before landing at 70 m.p.h. in the place where my ancestors used to take an afternoon stroll. 'Piece of cake,' they said. 'Pieces of me all over the park,' I rather thought, and turned an interesting shade of green.

The first part wasn't too bad, except when an uncharitable reporter stuck a microphone in front of my face, and said, 'Lord Bradford, it's a bit windy up there!'

'Yes, but I'm not,' I replied, lying through my teeth.

Then take-off, with my stomach doing a remarkably good impression of a cement-mixer. Up we soared. Though I was tightly adhered to the top of the plane, an overwhelming sense of insecurity and impending doom assaulted me, as mouth agape, I careered through the air. But I very quickly learned to keep my trap shut. When you're flying forwards at a speed of 100 m.p.h., the law of physics dictates that your companions in the stratosphere – a selection of flies, winged beetles and other creepy-crawlies – are hurtling backwards at a similar rate of knots. If you keep your mouth open, you begin to fulfil the function of an airborne whale shark, sifting the atmosphere of living debris. After several large flies had crashed into the back of my throat, I resolved to keep my lips well sealed.

It soon became clear that the helicopter had failed to materialize. Nevertheless, we had to perform a number of low passes over the runway for the benefit of the TV people, so that they'd have something to show for their efforts. This was all going to plan, as we merrily looped around the park, until my back started to trouble me. When the pain became intolerable, I gave the thumbs-down to the pilot and the plane made a fairly speedy landing, much to my relief. The ordeal was over, or so I thought. When we taxied up to the photographers to give them their last shot of the day, they had some unwelcome news of their own.

'Marvellous,' they said. 'You'll be pleased to learn that the helicopter has just arrived. Can you wait a second whilst we get on board it?'

So, gritting my teeth, we went up again. Trying my best to wave at the cameras as I had been instructed, and with my back stretched to breaking point, I circled the grounds three or four times. By this time, any enjoyment in the escapade had dried up for me. Every moment in the air was a moment of agony, qualified by the dreadful premonition that I might never walk again, or at least in the normal way. Landing came as sweet relief, signalling the end of a morning's well ventilated torture.

Dropping unsteadily to the ground, I reflected that the show had been a considerable success and well worth while despite my pain. With the ample press attendance, and the unprecedented format of the event, we should have achieved enough publicity to rescue the annual air display from its recent decline. Sadly, fate had other ideas.

That very night York Minster was struck by lightning and burnt down. Unsurprisingly, this dramatic and sad event monopolized the editorials on the following day, and my personal stunt only made it to page five of the *Wolverhampton Express and Star*, with brief exposure on the local Midlands TV news programme. Not what we had hoped and strived for.

Even this limited publicity, however, had the effect of attracting large crowds to the subsequent display. Most were rather keen to witness the antics of the flying Lord, which had been billed as a special event. 'Special' wasn't the word; I was looking forward to a repeat run, like a mass murderer anticipates the electric chair ... But I was prepared to endure the misery if the price was right. A multitude of paying visitors meant that it was.

Unfortunately, nature had yet to play its decisive role in wrecking the occasion. Not long after the start of the display, the coordinator for the 'Barnstormers' asked to have a word with me. 'I've got some bad news for you, I'm afraid,' he said. 'The cross-wind is extremely strong this afternoon, so we won't be able to carry anyone weighing over eight and a half stone. It just wouldn't be safe to take you.'

Toying with the idea of a crash diet – one that could remove forty pounds in under half an hour – I racked my brains for solutions to the aviational impasse. None came … none that wasn't eminently inappropriate anyway.

The situation became extremely embarrassing for me when the commentator announced over the loudspeaker system, 'Regrettably the Earl of Bradford cannot go up on the plane this afternoon, so Jane, of the daring "Barnstormers Flying Circus", is taking his place.'

The immediate reaction of the crowd was 'Lord Bradford's chickened out!' Given different circumstances I might well have chickened out, but they were wrong in this instance. 'If only they could have seen me at my finest hour,' I was thinking, so I got hold of the public address system, and tried to set the record straight. Judging from the sceptical reaction of the crowd, I'm not sure I did a very good job. Many of them went home thinking the Earl wasn't up to it. How tragic they never knew just how far 'up' I'd really been!

Running a pheasant shoot can be a hazardous business – there aren't many service industries which combine unpredictable revenue with the chance to get your head blown off by a customer. British shoots are, by and large, famed for their stringent safety codes. Participants are expected to behave and shoot in a certain manner – major transgressions generally result in ostracism, if not infamy. Regrettably, though, there are still people who forget what a lethal weapon a shotgun can be; they assume that because the gun has been designed for the shooting of pheasants, it can be waved about in the air, pointed in any direction, and treated with the casual disdain of a gardening implement. They are perilously wrong.

For many years we have hosted commercial shoots at Weston Park, with varying degrees of success. The greatest problems have arisen when dealing with certain parties from abroad who have either taken up the sport rather late in life, or are unaccustomed to shooting 'driven game', by which I mean birds flying towards them. (Many Americans, for instance, have only been quail or whitewing hunting. In both of these, the birds are 'walked up', then fired at as they go away from the guns. This is radically different from shooting high pheasants coming towards you over your head, and requires another kind of skill.)

In particular we will never forget a German shooting party that came to Weston three years in a row. They were mostly highly successful businessmen and industrialists, fielding the head of the German coal mines among their number. I have never come across such a ruthlessly competitive bunch. Distraught unless they managed to kill many more birds than they were actually paying for, they displayed a similar attitude to food and wine, putting away more sandwiches and scones in one afternoon than an entire brigade of Boy Scouts could ever hope to.

The quality of the guns was also suspect. Two of them shot quite beautifully, selecting only the fastest and most difficult birds. The rest blasted away indiscriminately, as though auditioning for a wildlife version of *Zulu Dawn*. After a while, they became more selective. They went for the kind of pheasant that most sportsmen would consider untouchable – the birds that waddles up to you slower than an armadillo, the bird that practically perches itself on the end of your barrels. Add to this a predilection for super-heavy 'Rottweil' cartridges, and most of the birds were rendered totally inedible or at least unrecognizable. The shoot deteriorated into a pointless 'pointing' exercise – just point your gun and shoot.

One year they included in their party a peculiarly inept shot. He wasn't just inaccurate or under-ambitious, he was downright dangerous. His bag on the second day included one pheasant, one hare, three beaters, and a loader. These last two he managed to pepper with exceeding accuracy. The pellets penetrated their clothing in the chest area, though luckily for them, the shot got no further, and the skin was only slightly bruised. We passed the moment off as tactfully as possible, but instructed his personal loader to keep an eye on the miscreant. If lives looked to be in jeopardy, he should wrestle the gun away from the man, using strong-arm tactics if necessary.

The following day fortunately passed without further incident, but after the last drive, the leader of the group came up to me. He looked unhappy about something, and burst into a complaining monologue, most of which was lost on me as his accent was very thick indeed. I did however catch his last remark, although I could scarcely credit it: '... Alzo, ve did not have such gut shootink today. Zer ver not enough beaters!'

I know that Germans are not renowned for their appreciation of the finer points of irony. But I couldn't believe that this national deficiency extended to powers of recall as well. I had to bite my tongue and just resisted saying: 'Well if you hadn't shot so many of them yesterday, you would have had more today!' You have to please the client.

Before I am unfairly accused of 'Basil Fawlty, German-bashing Syndrome', I should like to tell a story about Count Underberg, who was also part of this particular group. Generous to a fault, charming, and a superb shot, he arrived in a large shooting brake fitted with an extremely well stocked bar. Bottles of Dom Pérignon and a myriad of other drinks lined the boot of his smart estate car, in the spot where a parcel shelf is more usually found.

The weather was cold and crisp. At the end of the second drive when we stopped for a break, the Count began distributing a wide choice of warming tinctures for the guns, more normally the duty of the host.

Being of a naturally open nature, he didn't forget the beaters, and produced a cardboard box full of Underberg, a foul-tasting brew that has proved enormously successful, creating a fortune for their family. Its main application would appear to be in the curing of hangovers, although I would have thought it merely adds to the agony. In its country of origin, it is astoundingly popular, although that is no recommendation – the Spanish rave about Fernet Branca, a similar home product of abominable flavour. (Underberg comes in tiny dark bottles, and is freely available in Munich, if you feel tempted to try it.) The beaters were impressed by the Count's kindness to them. They gathered round the box eagerly, innocent to the punitive qualities of its contents, and received a small bottle each. Appreciation was most vocal, 'Thank you very much indeed, sir,' 'Come again next year, Guv,' and they settled down to enjoy their unexpected bonus.

Connoisseurs drink the whole thing in one go, which gets the experience over as quickly as possible. Sadly, the beaters did not know this. They started to sip the drink slowly, as though savouring a fine port. Within seconds it dawned on them that this was not the pleasant-tasting liqueur they had imagined. A barrage of spitting and cursing ensued. Their faces went rigid with revulsion.

The next day Count Underberg seemed genuinely surprised and disappointed that none of the beaters wished to repeat the experience. When the cardboard box came out of the car, they trotted off in the direction of the next drive well ahead of schedule.

Another party we hosted called themselves 'The Bombay Bicycle Club of Houston'. This sounded like great fun until we realized that the name was in fact a decoy, or at least an obscure euphemism. Far from being a cycling association, (there wasn't a bicycle mentioned all weekend), the group appeared to have only one thing in common. They were all American property developers with a penchant for the extra-marital.

The club was plainly an excuse to leave the wives behind, and bring along a selection of busty maidens – including on one occasion a celebrated former 'Playmate of the Year' who proved most popular with the (male) staff. These nymphs evidently fulfilled the function of decorative 'bed-warmers', although one girl in particular was less than ecstatic when she, belatedly, discovered the role required of her. She categorically refused to sleep in the same room as her 'intended', causing much embarrassment to the jilted individual, as you may imagine.

Only one member opted to import his wife with him, but as she was a stunning beauty he obviously felt safer having her around. This was an understandable attitude when you considered his almost unbelievable ugliness ... and it was his third marriage!

Entertaining a party of this kind has its ups and downs. On the one hand, they are less likely to cause a kerfuffle in the library after dinner, as they seem remarkably keen to retire to bed. On the other, they are lousy shots ... then again their minds are doubtless concentrated elsewhere.

Our beaters will certainly never forget the group a top Texan oilman brought to stay at Weston Park. He was patently a very prosperous man, but had the disturbing habit of reminding you of this fact every five minutes with an enthusiasm bordering on the messianic. Gordon Gekko would have felt intimidated in his presence.

He was the sort of man who has to do everything well, which was fortunate for us, for at least he could shoot. Sadly most of the rest of his party were incapable of hitting a barn door at ten paces.

At our top drive, 'The Rock', one guest fired seventy-two cartridges before he finally brought down a bird – the unluckiest bird in the world, we thought, as he was most likely aiming at the one in front. His shooting was, by any standards, breathtakingly poor, achieving a consistency of inaccuracy to be marvelled at.

But even this man couldn't compare in peril potential with the Texan's wife, who insisted on taking part. We had no problem with that, except she repeatedly raised her gun far too early before the birds were within firing distance. This meant that on certain drives where the ground was flat, the beaters found themselves staring down the barrels of her gun. At length they grew tired of toying with death in this way, and mutinied.

We were shooting 'The Quarry', a wood where the guns always stand close to the edge awaiting fast, escaping birds. Ten yards short of the end of the drive, the beaters inexplicably halted. They withdrew behind the nearest tree-trunk, waving white handkerchiefs in a frantic bid for surrender.

When I got on the radio to ask them what they thought they were doing, the note of terror was unmistakable: 'We're not f … ing coming out, until that f … ing woman puts her f … ing gun down.' Needless to say, the Texan's party chose never to return to Weston. We weren't entirely devastated.

Lord Lambton has long been one of the most distinguished shots in the country. A story told to the present Duke of Northumberland by his old gamekeeper concerns Lord Lambton out shooting one day.

He was at a very testing stand, and proceeded to go through a most uncharacteristic 'dry patch' in which his usual high standards of accuracy continued to elude him. After missing two birds in succession, the Lord flew into a rage, picked up both his guns, and threw them into the River Wear running nearby.

He cooled down after a while, and cooled down even more when he went wading into the river to retrieve his weapons. The water was so icy that he suffered from double pneumonia for the rest of the winter. There must be a moral there somewhere ...

Different nations have different shooting traditions. The British always form a single line and usually shoot birds coming towards them. The French are more relaxed, and have been known to stand in a circle and walk inwards, killing anything that moves. Americans are still less formal, and show remarkable imagination in their choice of weaponry. A double-barrelled 12-bore from Holland and Holland cannot really compete, blast for blast, with a state of the art Uzi semi-automatic, and they've cottoned on to this in Arizona. *Chacun à son goût* ...

But there is one bird which is unique to Britain, and so is the style in which it is shot. It is the red grouse, a tough little creature that has thrived in certain parts of this country despite its many natural and human predators.

After the 'Glorious Twelfth of August', avid sportsmen from around the world come in their droves to participate in the seasonal fray. There tends to be quite a ceremony about these occasions. Guns stand in 'butts', low screens constructed out of stones or cubes of peat cut from the moorland, and wait as the birds are driven over. Patience is a must.

A famous moor in Yorkshire hosted a party of varied nationalities one year, many of whom had not shot grouse before. When they arrived, the host took pains to explain the finer points, but felt that he should keep a very close eye the next day.

It was a brilliant morning as the team set out for the moor with the heather in bloom, the bees buzzing about their work, and the sheep quietly grazing on the hillside. The smells of the late summer, and the warmth of the sun, cheered the men as they plodded along, inducing an expectation of fine sport to follow.

When they reached the correct spot, the guns drew their numbers and lined out for the first drive on the side of the hill. The host took the precaution of positioning himself at the bottom, from where he could safely watch the guests, all except for a Frenchman whose butt was just out of sight.

Once the beaters had reached their starting point, the drive began. A flock of sheep, roused from their feeding by the noise and the waving of the flags, suddenly scattered, and came tumbling over the heather towards the guns. They were swiftly followed by large clouds of grouse, and the sound of whistling shot could soon be heard for miles around.

The host looked on with delight; the birds were flying well, he noted, for so early in the season, and the guests were performing with distinction. He noticed in particular that the end butt, occupied by the lone Frenchman, was getting plenty of good shooting – if his repeated cries of enthusiasm were anything to go by.

But he was cut short in his admirations by the apparition of a rotund figure who came tearing over the hillside. The man was running with a purpose, as his arms were flapping about wildly, and he could be heard yelling: 'Somebody stop that ruddy maniac now! Stop him!'

Recognizing him to be the local farmer, the host stood in amazement as the Wellington-shod Yorkshireman scrambled and bounded through the undergrowth in what appeared to be the direction of the far butt. The guns in turn lowered their weapons, and watched in silence.

With the shoot brought to an abrupt halt, the host decided that he must pursue the frenzied farmer, who had just disappeared over the brow of the hill. He gave chase, and gaining the incline, came upon a vision that stopped him in his tracks – the Frenchman standing in triumphant pose, surrounded by a collection of dead sheep, which he had obviously shot in preference to the much faster grouse. On seeing the shoot organizer, he raised his hands towards the sky and exclaimed: '*Ah, le sport, c'est magnifique! Les moutons sauvages sont superbes*!'

The farmer was down on the ground, his face in the heather, and could be heard whimpering: 'I can't believe it. He's shot me prize tup ram!'

The Frenchman, by no means bilingual, plainly saw this as some kind of commendation. He blushed with pride, and uttered the modest disclaimer, '*Non, pas du tout, pas du tout*!'

Similarly appalling was an incident involving an Italian gun on another moor. One of the British guests had brought along a particularly disobedient spaniel which, when the firing began, would get very excitable, rushing to and fro, and generally spoiling the drive.

Normally you would expect the owner to keep the dog tied to a stick in the butt, but if he did this the spaniel launched into such a cacophony of whining and howling that the gun simply couldn't concentrate. He had therefore developed his own novel solution, which was to take a few cartridges, remove the shot from them and replace it with salt.

Whenever the spaniel misbehaved, he fired one of these treated cartridges into the area where the mutt was causing havoc. The dog would let out a little yelp, and speed back to his master's feet, completely unharmed.

On the shoot in question, the spaniel decided to collect a crossing bird that its owner had brought down well in front of the butts. Horrified at the chaos this would create, the gun reached for one of his special cartridges, and fired at the dog, which duly squealed and started to head back.

Sadly an Italian sportsman in the next door butt got the wrong idea, and let off two shots. The dog rolled over and died.

The owner turned in fury to his Continental neighbour, who jubilantly declared: 'Ha ha, you not so hot a shot, you missa the dog, I hit him.'

Lest we give the impression that it is only 'guests' who create problems on shoots, Lord Mountgarret's account of his unfortunate experience with a hot air balloon might redress the balance.

'Out grouse shooting one day a hot-air balloon appeared, floating 20 feet above the moor on the last drive of the day, completely ruining the shooting and scattering the birds in all directions. Taking the entirely reasonable action, I fired three warning shots across the bows to encourage it to go away, but of course neither aiming at the balloon nor hitting it. To have given the proverbial two barrels might have been better understood, but the pilot seemed not to notice the early warning, so a third shot was required.

'However the authorities were not impressed and I landed

in a certain amount of trouble.'

Tersely put, but not the whole story.

Some years later, the same balloon reappeared over a neighbouring moor and crashed into a wall near the keeper's house. Following this incident the owner of the moor received a telephone call from the unfortunate balloonist. 'I really must protest. Your gamekeeper was no help whatsoever. He came out of his house, looked at me for a few moments, then disappeared back inside. He could at least have offered a hand!'

This information noted, the owner went down to see his employee, and asked him to explain. The gamekeeper gave a sly look and commented laconically, 'I've got better things to do, sir, than pick up one of Lord Mountgarret's runners.' (A runner is a wounded game bird.)

The 10th Duke of Northumberland was a great fox-hunting man and Master of the Percy Hunt for many years. On his Surrey estate, there is a small cottage in the middle of the woods, which was let to a lady who took in orphaned animals, including foxes. This woman lived in constant fear that the Duke would find out and have her evicted for harbouring vermin.

One day, about five years after she moved in, there came a knock on the cottage door. Looking out of the window, the animal lover spotted the Duke's agent. She rushed over to close the sitting room off from the kitchen, and hesitantly invited the visitor in.

'Terribly sorry to bother you,' he said, 'but my car's got stuck in the mud. Could I use your telephone?' The woman said that of course he could, and politely offered to make him a cup of coffee.

A few minutes later, as they stood in the kitchen talking

about this and that, a fearful commotion erupted in the sitting room. It was followed by a great crash as a door flew open and a fox dashed through the kitchen, skidded twice on the polished floor, and burst out through the cat flap.

The agent shook his head in disbelief, then looked inquiringly at the tenant.

'Er, yes ...', she improvised. 'One of my dogs actually ... little known breed, you know ... practically extinct!'

The agent seemed doubtful, and his suspicions were confirmed when the fox crept back through the cat flap and took up position near the radiator at the far end of the kitchen. It watched the visitor steadily, eyes gleaming in the afternoon half-light.

'My God,' muttered the man to himself, 'wait till the Duke hears about this!'

The woman turned to him in anguish. 'Oh please don't tell His Grace!' she cried. 'I love it here, and if he finds out he'll have me evicted!'

'Have you evicted?' the agent laughed. 'Good gracious no – he'll be tickled pink! I should imagine he'll want to come and see the fox himself.'

Sadly, the Duke died before he had the opportunity to visit the cottage, but the fox continues to live there to this day.

We have hosted one of the Sunday 'Spectator Stages' of the RAC Rally about fifteen times. These are the moneyspinners for the organizers – not only are they sponsored, but the public also pay to attend, which brings in valuable revenue for subsequent rallies. Whilst the onlookers find the events most entertaining, the competitors dislike them heartily, referring to them as 'The Mickey Mouse Stages', since the course is often excessively fiddly, involving artificial obstacles, hairpin bends and countless chicanes.

The event coordinators like to use the grounds of stately homes, such as Chatsworth, Tatton or Weston, as well as large municipal parks like Clumber, near Nottingham, and Sutton in Birmingham, because they provide plenty of thrills and spills within a reasonably contained viewing area. The drivers are less thrilled, as they are at the mercy of experimenting aristocrats, who, in the interests of crowd attendance, like to make the track as exciting as possible.

Generally these events are a huge success, exhilarating to behold and great fun to host (it's not every day you get a chance to watch high-quality mechanical engineering being thrashed around your front lawn by the world's top rally drivers) and we feel most lucky to be selected as a venue. But as in any public spectacle involving fast-moving vehicles, you must expect a motoring fiasco from time to time. Our time came on one memorable occasion when the entire Vauxhall team came to grief at our specially constructed 'Water Splash'.

We had created the splash ourselves some years previously by damming a small stream that ran through the park. It was all professionally built, I hasten to add, with tarmac on the road, and concrete on the brook bed. We thought that it would add an extra dimension to the rally at Weston, and for the first few years it did. One year, though, it succeeded in bringing the event to a virtual standstill. Usually the water was about six inches deep, but on this particular day it was two inches higher than normal by dint of an incorrectly positioned plank.

Derek Bell, a past winner of the Le Mans 24-Hour Race and an acclaimed sports car champion, was due to make an appearance in the Vauxhall team and the organizers were naturally thrilled by the publicity that this would bring. Camera crews turned up *en masse* to interview the great man, and asked him to predict where he might come in the RAC Rally. 'Well, I think I'll do all right,' he replied, exuding confidence from every pore.

The Sunday arrived, Weston being one of the early stages to

fit in with the TV schedules. Off went Derek, zooming round the course at breakneck speed. He was doing better than 'all right' until he encountered the water splash, which brought his car from thirty to zero in an instant. The thing just stopped, and seized up completely. He tried to restart the vehicle – not a spark of life. The poor old champion was forced to make the most ignominious of exits – heaving himself from the car, he dropped into eight inches of water, and with the help of several marshals, pushed the stalled Vauxhall out of the dam.

The same fate awaited all the other cars in the team. They got to the splash, but that's as far as they got – something to do with the air intakes being too low, I think. A bad day for Vauxhall's motor technicians, then. Still, we expected them to thank us for highlighting this obvious design fault. Sadly, they didn't see it that way.

As for Mr Bell, he retired from this particular form of motor sport – permanently.

Lamport Hall in Northamptonshire was home to the Isham family from 1560 to 1976. The 10th Baronet of Lamport, Sir Charles Isham, is credited with the invention of the garden gnome which he introduced to his own Italian garden and the nation at large in the mid nineteenth century. May he be blessed eternally for that act of creation!

Recorded in history as a charming eccentric, he was certainly rather forgetful. He was also a keen rider and kept two hunters; one steady and reliable, the other fiery and temperamental. Though not a huge fan of hunting himself – unsurprising really, as he founded the Vegetarian Society – the Baronet did feel obliged to show his face from time to time at the local hunt.

He was once seen galloping across the hunting field

towards an imposing brush hedge when, inexplicably, he stopped, dismounted and walked around to the front of the horse. He stood there for a couple of seconds and, remounting, proceeded to jump the obstacle in the usual way.

At lunch later that day, he was asked to explain his bizarre behaviour. 'Well you see, I needed to know which horse I was on,' he replied.

Guests

(paying and otherwise)

It is often assumed that because you own a large house and have a title you are intimately familiar with every member of the Royal Family, have them over regularly for tea and crumpets, even take baths together. I cannot speak for every peer of the realm, but I for one don't go fishing with Prince Charles, nor do I swap recipe tips with the Queen Mother. I am as likely to join the royal entourage on an inter-continental cruise holiday as to represent my country at the next world figure skating championships – not very.

On a windy November afternoon some years ago, I paid a visit to the local barber. It was a typically quiet Saturday, most of the staff were off, and I was preparing myself – mentally as well as tonsorially – for the first stage of the RAC Lombard Rally which we were hosting at Weston the following morning.

I can usually expect tranquillity at the hairdresser's. Short of a volcanic eruption in the library, or a stealth bomber landing on the front lawn, news from the house is, for these precious moments anyway, shielded from me. It is a time for reflection, contemplation and a little local gossip.

So the blood rushed to my face when they relayed a message to me from my wife, who urgently required my presence at home. What could this mean? Horrifying scenes flickered before my eyes – a convention of Hell's Angels camping in the park, the head chef threatening to throw himself from the banisters whilst clutching a bottle of cooking brandy, Michael Winner arriving for a surprise visit …

I leapt from the barber's chair mid-trim, apologized for my behaviour, and shot off back home. My wife was waiting for me there. 'Richard, we have a distinguished visitor wanting to look round the hall this afternoon.'

I breathed a sigh of relief. This discounted one of my theories at least.

'Leonora Lichfield has just rung from Shugborough. Princess Margaret is staying with them at the moment and she's asking to see Weston.'

Gulping, 'What, today?' I paused to consider the complexities of the situation. On the one hand, a prominent member of the *Royal* family wanted to view *our* family home, a request I could hardly refuse, even if I wanted to. On the other, three-quarters of our staff – including the tour guides – were off duty, probably holed up in the local pub, enjoying a weekend pre-prandial drink. A tidal wave wouldn't shift them. What chance did I stand?

'Okay, tell Leonora that we'd be delighted to receive her.'

Delighted? Not exactly. Deep down, I was experiencing the same kind of anxiety I used to feel at preparatory school when, summoned by the headmaster to explain my part in a particularly rewarding water fight, I'd stand outside his office hoping to avoid a painful encounter with a size 14 rubber-soled running shoe.

Still, I thought to myself, two things had significantly changed since my student days – first, authority figures were no longer likely to set about me with a specially constructed Dunlop product; secondly, my rhetorical skills had improved. I'd given guided tours before and prided myself on an ability to enthuse, even amuse the most imperious visitor. Surely, Princess Margaret would be no exception …

The impossibly long, black Daimler limousine swung into the park at two-thirty precisely. I had managed to assemble all the staff at my disposal in front of the house, and with grave misgivings on my part and great excitement on theirs, we watched the royal car approach. It crawled towards us ominously, a stately-home-seeking missile undeviating in its course and devastating in impact. I straightened my tie, then tightened it. I adjusted my collar. If this went on for much longer, the host-cum-guide was going to need urgent asphyxiation treatment. I told myself to relax, and settled into a paroxysm of one-legged shoe polishing.

At length, the Princess got out. She was not particularly dressed for a state occasion, but in simple garb – well, simple if you ignored the conspicuous opulence of her black mink coat – and this comforted me momentarily. I was able to sail through the usual procedure of greeting and introductions, with all the staff lined up to be presented.

As we entered the front hall, she lit up the first of many cigarettes and I began my talk on the history of the house, starting with the obligatory acknowledgement: 'Weston Park is, of course, as nothing when set against the magnificence of Britain's grandest stately homes, such as Blenheim or Chatsworth,' carefully avoiding any comparison with the majesty of Buckingham Palace, Kensington Palace, Balmoral or Sandringham. 'Nevertheless, it might please you to learn some of its charming idiosyncrasies …'

I was gliding along sweetly enough, and on the point of making a witty little observation about the origins of the name Weston-under-Lizard (Old English 'Lazar Yard', meaning 'leper colony') and the fact that I still had the full use of my limbs, when the target of my discourse took sudden flight, and hurried off from the hall in the direction of the main staircase.

My speech abruptly terminated. This was not what I'd been expecting. Something must be wrong when a member of the Royal Family feels her only salvation lies in immediate retreat. I followed the Princess further into the house, and speedily caught up with her.

She had reached the tapestry room, and was surveying the impressive Gobelin tapestries. She continued to smoke, but seemed reluctant to use her lips for any other purpose – like speech, for example.

The ball was firmly in my court; so I resumed service, ashtray held in the style of an ancient Egyptian dancer waiting for the next flick. 'As you may know, Ma'am, this set is one of the few remaining in private hands. After more than 200 years, it is still in the ownership of the family that commissioned it ...'

I'd got no further than the second sentence when, once again, my guest took to her heels and disappeared through a door. This left me in the uncomfortable position of delivering a historical dissertation to the rest of the group – who were suitably amused – and a fast dissolving trail of cigarette smoke.

It also got me thinking. Either the Princess found my monologue lethally tedious, but was too polite to say so; or she was suffering from an acute bout of hypertension. I favoured the latter naturally, but felt compelled to give chase. I found the fugitive staring at some of the very fine china in the drawing room. It was on this subject that she chose to get technical, fatal for me as I knew almost nothing about the porcelain in the house.

I considered honesty the best policy, and owned up to my ignorance. But I couldn't just leave it there, so I tried to steer the debate towards topics which might prove more fertile.

She paused in front of the exceptional portrait of Lady Wilbraham, her eyebrows arched inquisitively. I took this as my cue: 'Your Royal Highness, this picture is rather unique in that ...'

'Rather unique?' my companion interjected, the eyebrows by this stage an unimportant distance from her hairline.

'Er, yes, Ma'am ...'

'Surely, it is either unique or it is not,' the Princess contended. 'You cannot have gradations of uniqueness.'

Quivering with embarrassment, I tried to find an answer to this grammatical *faux pas*. It did not come, so I nodded frantically in acquiescence. I was back in the headmaster's office ...

After this, one of the few exchanges of the tour, I decided to hang up my orator's gown, and allowed the visitor to continue with minimal further commentary on my part. I didn't fancy another grammatical pummelling, and to be honest my brain had ceased to function. We completed the circuit in almost total silence, and our goodbyes were relieved, I'm sure, on both sides. Strangely, I found myself looking forward to the simple joys of hosting a world-famous motor rally.

When the Queen paid a visit to Syon House in 1993, following a fund-raising event held in the grounds for cancer research, the present Duke of Northumberland was told by her equerries that she should not be offered any tea or cakes as she was on a diet. When finally the Queen arrived, and the Duke saw everyone sipping from their cups and munching away happily, he said to his honoured guest: 'Are you sure that you wouldn't like some refreshment, Ma'am?'

She looked confused and a little dismayed by the question, replying promptly: 'Of course I would, that's why I'm here.'

It can be more than a little embarrassing when the equerries don't get it quite right.

One American tourist at Syon was saying what a lovely position the house was in, when he paused for reflection, looked up at an aircraft flying overhead and said, 'Still, it's a pity that they built it so close to the airport.'

(Syon House, of course, preceded the building of Heathrow airport by some 600 years.)

The Great Conservatory at Syon is often hired out for parties, particularly wedding receptions. The scheme has proved so popular, with the bookings coming in thick and fast, that the first question asked by the staff of any prospective client is, 'Have you got a set date in mind?'

On one occasion they were met with the rather piqued answer, 'Well, no, not really. She isn't dead yet! I want to book a wake!'

An American film producer was walking through the state rooms at Syon. In one small corner there is a large framed painting of the Percy family tree, under which there is the title: 'The Genealogy of the Dukes'.

The producer, who was rushing to catch up with the rest of the tour party, must have misread the sign, as he was heard to exclaim by the Duke: 'Good God – what does that say? The Gynaecology of the Dykes?'

Contributions from Alnwick Castle, one of the Duke of Northumberland's family residences

A guide overheard two middle-aged ladies discussing the merits of the pictures: 'I do love the Titans, but you really can't beat the Cannelonis.'

On examining the 1760 Gainsborough portrait of one of the Drummond ancestors, a visitor was heard to remark: 'I wonder if he was a relation of Bulldog?'

A party touring the castle recently inquired of a guide whether the Percys were giants. The guide asked them why they wanted to know this – the reply was, 'Well the mirrors are so high above the fireplaces.'

In the state dining room hangs a painting of the 5th Duke of Northumberland, signed by the artist, G. Pope. One visitor was overheard muttering, 'Goodness gracious me! I never knew they had a Pope in the family!'

We have many requests for party visits to Weston Park, but one of the more exotic ones – as it turned out – came from an amateur photographic society based in Bournemouth. Fairly specific in their requests, they wanted to take pictures of the house, but only in the bedrooms. They asked for changing facilities for their 'models' which we unquestioningly laid on, assuming the 'sitters' would need plenty of space to clothe themselves in intricate, period costume.

The group arrived on a Sunday morning, and towards midday I rang through to our head guide to check everything was running smoothly. She sounded agitated. 'Oh dear, I don't think you're going to be very pleased.'

'Not pleased?' I inquired. 'Why?'

Her embarrassment coursing down the telephone line, she stammered disapprovingly, 'Well, the girls are not wearing much in the way of clothing, my Lord.'

My suspicions aroused, I tore over to the house and came upon what looked like the beginnings of a *Sunday Sport* photo spectacular. A selection of young, and not so young, women were parading in the upper chambers of Weston with barely a gym-slip between them. I am no expert on such matters, but I believe it is the custom among amateur photographers to give their models a motivational pep-talk prior to the taking of pictures. Thus it was that the men behind the cameras, oblivious to my presence, began making various suggestions whilst the women sashayed provocatively down the corridors as they prepared for a state of complete déshabillé.

Two visions – both terrifying – shot through my mind: a caption in a saucy tabloid reading 'Wendy and Wilhelmina Get Wanton at Weston!', and my head being hung from the battlements by the trustees of the Weston Park Foundation.

Immediately I ordered the society out of the house, and at length they left, muttering discontentedly to themselves as though I'd spoiled a particularly good party. I wasn't too concerned, having discovered to my relief that no photographs had actually been taken. I'd nipped them in the bud, and prevented a major catastrophe.

The next day a story appeared in the *Sun* with the headline, 'Wild Earl Blows His Topless!' and accompanying pictures. I didn't have to think too hard to work out the source of this particular gem. A woman 'scorned' perhaps?

The report in the newspaper moved one of our neighbours to pen a limerick in commemoration of the incident. It read:

> Bare-bosomed girls look their best on
> The beds in the guest rooms at Weston
> Are photographs cheaper
> For a bawdy-house keeper?
> It depends on which boob she's caressed on!

Thank you for that, Alan.

Around 1750 Sir Marmaduke Wyvill decamped to Ireland with his whole household, leaving instructions for huge repairs to be carried out on his large Elizabethan home at Constable Burton. On his eventual return, he sent some footmen ahead to check out the situation. They soon came back and reported to him that they were unable to find the house!

Sir Marmaduke galloped on and found that, owing to some apparent failure of communication, his house had been razed to the ground!

John Carr of York was called for and instructed to build a new mansion, which resulted in an extremely fine and beautiful Palladian house; anyone who has seen pictures of the original Elizabethan structure will appreciate that the present incumbents have been fortunate indeed!

The gardens at Constable Burton, home of Maggie and Charles Wyvill, are open to the public from the first Bank Holiday in May and for the next six months. One year, however, they got rather behind in their preparation work, so Maggie was dragged out to do some weeding.

Looking somewhat out of place as a gardener – beautiful blonde ladies are usually seen in more decorous roles – she was viciously tearing away at a particularly obstinate patch of weeds when two doughty Yorkshire matrons in obligatory country tweeds, who had arrived rather early, came up to her. 'Oh dear,' they said, 'that seems like very hard work. Do they pay you well?'

'Not really,' responded Maggie. 'But I do get to sleep with the boss.'

Silence followed for a few seconds in which the two ladies exchanged a series of startled looks. Then they choroused, 'How nice,' and strode off, muttering conspiratorially to each other.

During one of the grand parties that the Wyvills host at Constable Burton, they had an unexpected and unwelcome additional guest – one member of their large colony of bats. This creature decided to join them as they were relaxing after a superb dinner with the result that eight VIPs, all in their dinner jackets, began running around the drawing room with fishing nets, in a farcical effort to ensnare the poor thing.

The situation took a turn for the worse, when one of the guests appeared with a gun in his hand. Fortunately Maggie had had the foresight by this time to open the windows wide, and, mercifully for the Wyvills and their drawing room, the bat was able to make a quick exit.

Sir Thomas Ingilby, owner of Ripley Castle in North Yorkshire, writes:

Over the years we have received some peculiar requests at Ripley. One of the more bizarre came from a German author, temporarily resident in London, asking us to send him some dust in an envelope (which he enclosed). He said he was gathering dust from museums throughout Europe in order to produce a travelling show, would you believe, as well as a book on the subject.

He explained, 'My purpose in this undertaking is conceptual: Dust as a biblical metaphor, as a literary and artistic symbol of fleetingness and finality; dust as a tangible token of possible associations of ideas ... I would appreciate your accompanying comment on the subject of Dust.'

What a strange fellow! Talk about being treated like dirt.

The late arrival of pre-booked tours always leads to upset,

but we had to smile when one particular group of nuns arrived at the castle very late, apologizing profusely. Their minibus had broken down en route from Fountains Abbey to Ripley, and all attempts by its occupants and various good samaritans to establish the cause had come to nought.

After some time the nuns decided that they would seek assistance from someone with an all-encompassing knowledge of motor cars and knelt down by the busy roadside in suppliant prayer. When the driver turned the ignition key, the engine started up first time. This is certainly the only time that we have had a miracle on the Road to Ripley, and it has convinced me that if only my faith were stronger, I could cancel my AA subscription and save myself a fortune.

In the large drawing room of the castle we have a life-sized statue of 'Venus Emerging from the Bath', an eighteenth-century piece from the workshops of Antonio Canova. It shows the goddess semi-naked, holding a robe loosely in front of her. On two occasions I have been asked by American visitors, 'Is that the Princess of Wales?' On a third memorable occasion I was asked if it was my wife.

All stately home owners tend to dread Bank Holidays. Certainly, the extra large crowds are most welcome, but the additional wear and tear – not just to buildings but to dispositions – is sometimes less so. Worst of all, these always seem to be the days when things go wrong.

Forde Abbey in Dorset – originally a Cistercian Monastery founded in 1140 – was converted to a private house during the mid seventeenth century and is now the home of Mark Roper.

After a successful Bank Holiday a few years ago, Mark Roper was walking round, congratulating everyone on an agreeably smooth performance, when an agitated man came bursting into the tea room. Catching his breath, he just managed to get out: 'Please help! I've lost my daughter!'

This is not an especially unusual occurrence. Staff are forever retrieving bewildered children from far corners of the estate. In fact, they have perfected a simple routine that clicks into gear whenever a child is missing, which is almost daily.

But on this occasion it took some time to piece together the tale from the breathless visitor. At length they learned that the 'child', who was in fact nineteen years old, had a fondness for the music of church bells. They also discovered that a wedding had been taking place in a neighbouring village that morning, and that in all likelihood the wandering damsel had set off in the direction of the merry peals. She had evidently got lost on the way.

Mark immediately postponed his supper. Prising the house guests away from their gin and tonics, all were dispatched to scour the highways and byways. But to no avail: eventually Mark had to swallow his pride and call in the local constabulary.

By this time the girl's father had become extremely upset. Only by taking regular doses from Mark's whisky bottle was he able to calm himself, and the bottle was fast emptying. An unpleasant scene looked likely ...

In the nick of time, someone spotted a Panda car coming at high speed down the drive. The driver seemed to be steering his vehicle in an unusual way – with his head half out of the window, he was gasping for air like a demented goldfish.

Mark and his staff rushed out to greet the policeman, who was just getting out of his Panda. As he did so, a most unholy stench washed over the assembled company: the unmistakable reek of cow manure.

The constable didn't look too happy. It transpired that the missing girl had in fact fallen into what our legislators now call a 'slurry lagoon' on her way to church, and that he had

had to rescue her.

A few days later the local Inspector came to call. From the way in which he refused the proferred libation it was obvious that he meant business, and that Mark was in for an embarrassing interview. 'You will appreciate, sir,' the police officer began, 'that we are woefully short of manpower. However, we are willing to accept certain privations in the course of our duties. Nevertheless I do feel that we should be able to draw the line at having to rescue young maidens from middens.'

Having said his piece, he made an abrupt but dignified exit.

Charles Clive-Ponsonby-Fane took on a monumental task when, in 1975, he decided to open up the family home, Brympton d'Evercy, a mansion in Somerset with a seventeenth-century south front and Tudor west front. Previously, the house had been a private school, and after many years of abuse at the hands of destructive children, it needed plenty of restoration. Nowadays it has prize-winning gardens and, unusually, its own vineyard.

One fine weekend Charles Clive-Ponsonby-Fane invited his sister, Isobel, to come and help plant the vineyard. Once they had started work, they began reminiscing, as siblings tend to do, and recalled happy childhood memories of their long school holidays, of the house and how it had been in times gone by; and how peaceful and quiet it had once more become.

It was a sweltering day, and as they worked on, they shed various layers of clothing. It seemed perfectly natural – they were totally alone and expecting nobody. All of a sudden, Isobel let out a shriek of horror. 'My God!' she cried. 'What the hell is that?'

'Christ!' said Charles quickly, though inaccurately, and scampered to find his trousers.

In through the front gates was nosing an enormous bright yellow charabanc. It eased its way along the drive and came to rest on the forecourt at the front of the house, hissing and puffing like some vast asthmatic monster. With a final gasp the coach door opened and out popped a Mrs Tiggywinkle figure.

The sight of two rather ponderous beings, darting furtively amongst the weeds as they try to garner both their respectability and a few crucial nether garments, might usually be expected to have an adverse effect on a little old lady. Not this time – she took it all in her stride, and advanced at speed towards the compromised duo.

Charles had not been particularly successful in his trouser hunt, so wearing little more than an uneasy smile, he sallied forth to meet the anonymous visitor. 'Good afternoon,' he said. 'Can I help you at all?'

'Good afternoon,' replied the woman, in a firm voice. 'Yes, I hope you can. You must be … ' She paused to refer to the mountain of printed paper she had clutched under one arm. 'You must be the owner, yes?'

'Well, yes,' returned the half-naked Charles, a little uncertain as to where this conversation was leading. 'That's about the rub of it.'

'Oh, good. We've come to see you!' said Mrs Tiggywinkle, with a curious emphasis on the last pronoun.

'You have?'

'Yes, of course. I understand that your house and gardens are open to the public. Well, we booked the coach and now we're here!'

'Yes, you see the problem is … ' Charlie managed to stammer, before he was sharply interrupted.

'There are fifty-two of us. We're from the Gardening Club. We're all keen gardeners, you know,' came the trilling cry.

'I do?'

'Yes. I'm going to ask the coach driver to blow his horn at 5.30 this afternoon. When he does, that's our signal to climb on board and go home,' said the amateur gardener, as if giving orders for the commencement of battle. 'But first,' and here she became a little coy, though not much, 'would you mind pointing me in the direction of the ladies' loo?'

The owner of Brympton d'Evercy looked at his feet, took a few deep breaths, then began slowly and deliberately: 'Now then ... First let me say how delighted and honoured we are to welcome so many worthy gardeners to our home. But I'm afraid things are not what they seem. The house and grounds ... ' Charles stopped mid-sentence. He'd suddenly noticed that the yellow monster was creaking and wobbling. Blurred shapes – hundreds of them, or so it seemed – were moving about inside. Then they got off.

An army of cultivators – most of them elderly, a small proportion positively geriatric – filed over the forecourt towards the unwitting Charles, who could only stand his ground, and watch in amazement.

'Good afternoon, sir,' said the first wizened old horticulturist, as he passed by.

'Good day, sir,' said the second cheerfully, going the same way.

'Most grateful, sir.'

'Very kind, sir.'

'Lovely afternoon, isn't it, sir?'

They were uniformly delightful he had to concede. But they were mistaken, badly mistaken.

Charles was shaken out of his reveries by the now familiar, confident voice. 'So, then,' she asked, fumbling in her Midland Bank money bag. 'What do I owe you?'

Charles felt this was his chance: 'Look, you don't understand. The house is empty; we have no ladies' loos, no tea rooms, and no guides. We're not ready yet. I couldn't possibly take your money,' he said, despairingly.

This didn't have quite the effect he imagined it would. Expecting a sea of crestfallen faces, he got a whole new flood of gardeners marching past, and a whole new wave of 'Afternoon, sir's. They were still exiting the charabanc in droves – the lady had said fifty-two, hadn't she? More like five hundred and two, he thought.

By this point, he really felt that he had to get it all sorted out before the whole situation became hopelessly out of hand. He turned to Mrs Tiggywinkle, but she had vanished. In fact, they had all disappeared. By any standards it is a large house, and the gardens extensive, but fifty-two gardeners seemed to have vanished into thin air, just like that.

'Isobel,' he said, since she was the only person still around. 'Do something! Please!' But Isobel just stood there, clutching her sides from the uncontrollable laughter that had stricken her.

Then suddenly the gardeners reappeared and swarmed everywhere. Like ants crawling over an old, abandoned apple core, they were upstairs, downstairs, in the cellar, and up the attic. As soon as Charles managed to corner two or three in a far bedroom, and usher them down and out the front hall, he'd find them, only a few minutes later, in some other distant corner of the house, poking into doors, cupboards, passages and pantries.

He must have said it a hundred times – 'No, madam, not in there, it's private!'

'Oh, sir, not to worry. I was only looking for the ladies' loos.'

'But, madam, this was a boys' school. We have no ladies' loos!'

Charles had forgotten how many doors there were in the house that could be left open, how many lights that could be left on, and how many outbuildings that could be penetrated ...

He had never thought of charabanc designers as being

particularly musical, but on that day the note of the coach horn was the sweetest of his life and, like the Pied Piper of Hamelin, it had the desired effect. Out they came, tumbling from coal shed, potting shed, tool shed, bedroom, bathroom, library. Chattering to each other as they hopped back on to the bus, with the ever efficient Mrs Tiggywinkle checking them off her list. When they were all safely accounted for, she turned and thanked Charles warmly. 'Oh thank you, sir, we have enjoyed ourselves so much, this our first visit to Forde Abbey.' And with that she climbed on to the yellow monster, which roared into life.

'Wait a minute,' said Charles, trying to make his voice heard above the noise of the engine. 'This isn't Forde Abbey – it's Brympton d'Evercy!' Nobody heard him – the gardeners shot away in a great blue cloud of dust and diesel fumes.

Slowly, the rumble died down and peace settled once again. As they gently plodded back to the vineyard, utterly exhausted, Isobel turned to her brother and said. 'Charles, do you really want to open your house to the public?'

Charles Clive-Ponsonby-Fane sent me some more Somerset tales

I was not at all worried that a particular bus was still parked by the gates a little after the normal departure time. Nor, when the hour came to lock up and the bus still hadn't moved, was I much concerned. I should have been.

As is my custom, I wandered down to talk to the driver, who is generally kind enough to lean on the horn for a few seconds and summon his group from the house. When I got to the coach, I was surprised to find that the driver had himself absconded.

'They must be in the tea rooms,' I thought, and walked over – no driver, no passengers. 'In the vineyard, then?' – no. 'In the house still?' – nobody.

This was a mystery. There was only one other place on the estate that I hadn't checked – the Cider Museum. But it had been closed for several hours and, besides, the staff were now off duty; I couldn't see why that particular spot should yield up an errant driver and his charges. Unless …

I opened the heavy, oak door, and peered into the gloom. 'Oh, hello, squire,' a great voice boomed out from the mire. 'Find yourself a seat, I was just telling my friends about Jethro Bull. Now Jethro worked for my uncle, on my mother's side, you understand … '

I had found the driver. There he was, like a one-man Somerset cabaret act, sitting on one corner of the cider press recounting stories from his childhood, surrounded by a gaggle of admiring passengers. But that wasn't the main problem.

In the course of his performance he had hit upon an ingenious wheeze which allowed him and his audience free and regular access to the cider supply. By emphasizing the more thrilling aspects of his history with a sudden jerk of the legs, the driver was able to knock the tap of the barrel nearest to him, which would release its contents into a vast, strategically positioned drinking horn.

When the time came for the amateur comedian to sample his (eighth? – he'd obviously been at this for some time) drink, he picked up the vessel, pondered it for a while, then turned to me in mock-astonishment. 'Oh dear, surr,' he said, not sounding remotely contrite, 'we seem to have sprung a leak.'

By way of a great favour to me, he observed that it was a pity to waste such good cider. He then took a monumental swig and passed the horn round. The passengers seemed equally anxious that none should be wasted, and all helped to drain the flagon. The horn was then neatly returned to the same spot under the barrel, and the driver resumed his oration. 'You know, I'm minded of a local man named Sam Axe, towering fellow with the thirst of a dragon ...'

I felt I had to interrupt. 'Yes, Mr Driver, I'm sure we're all keen to learn about Sam Axe and his amazing drinking abilities, but I think it's time you were on your way. The house, and that includes its cider supply, is now closed to the public.'

The driver, cut short in his latest riveting monologue, looked up at me in confusion. Playing the audience to a tee, he adopted the expression of a small child – one who has just been told that his birthday party is to be cancelled. The passengers, sensing his pain, issued a collective and disappointed, 'Aaah ...'

Luckily, the driver could tell from my impatient stare that I wasn't in the mood for pantomime. With a reluctant sigh, he heaved himself off the press, mumbled an obligatory, 'As you wish, surr,' and tottered off out of the door and into the darkness, followed by his flushed flock.

Just as the bus was finally about to leave, the sozzled driver leaned out of his window, and flashed me a wicked grin. 'Stand well back, surr,' he shouted above the roar of the engine. 'This bus do be runnin' on cider!'

A series of badly executed gear changes, and much crunching of gravel under tyre, could not quite drown out the boisterous strains of 'Land of Hope and Glory' that hung upon the air as the party plotted its meandering course down the drive.

The following was overheard on the gate: 'Good afternoon, sir.'

'How much then?'

'For two adults and two children, that will be three pounds please, sir.'

'What? I don't want to buy the bleeding place!'
'No, sir. That's ten pence extra.'

An elderly lady bustled into the gift shop and explained how thrilled she was that the house was so old ... 'And I do hope that you're still using those lovely pounds, shillings and pence!'

When Muhammad Ali came to visit Alnwick Castle, owned by the Dukes of Northumberland, he must have been very impressed with what he saw. He gave a signed photograph of himself to the 10th Duke, and asked him in a loud voice, 'So, how much does this place cost?'

The present Duke received a fax one day from his agent in the north. The missive bemused him because it read like an excerpt from an Alastair MacLean novel. Apparently, a group of men working for a Colombian drugs cartel, had orders to attack the National Gallery, Windsor Castle and Alnwick Castle.

The criminals would be using two cars, full to the brim with revolvers, grenades and heavy automatic weaponry. They had orders to assault the aforementioned places and steal the paintings inside – at any cost. The operation was to take place within the next two weeks, and at Windsor and Alnwick the combined forces of the police and army were to be put on full alert.

The source of the agent's information was the National Gallery, which had recently had some intruders. A car had been stopped and some people arrested. Inside the car the police had found details of the planned raids, an inventory of the military hardware to be used, and the rough dates for the attacks. The police had learned everything from this single vehicle which the gang had intended to use as a get-away car after the assault on the Gallery because, sadly for them, the raiders had overlooked one thing – London's stringent parking laws. Their car was clamped whilst they were inside the National Gallery, and their plans – all three of them – discovered.

On reading the fax, the Duke was relieved to see how such a potentially dangerous plot had been foiled by a commonplace parking offence. On this occasion he had reason to be gratified for the unstinting work of London's tireless traffic wardens!

It was a summer's evening shortly before the wedding of Prince Charles and Lady Diana Spencer. Jean Starkie was resting her feet in the garden of her home, Gaulden Manor, feeling rather tired and disagreeable, when she saw two figures approaching in the middle distance. This puzzled her somewhat as the hour was quite late, and the house about to be closed up for the day. But more intriguing were the couple themselves. The woman brandished a large white parasol, whilst the man was carrying a Gladstone bag – strange accoutrements for a historic tour, Jean thought, and she rushed in to warn her husband.

'James, two people are coming towards the house. The man looks just like a burglar, he's got a funny bag under his arm, and you've heard all those stories about stately homes being robbed in this area. Be very careful – insist that he leaves his bag in the hall, if they want to look round the house.'

Later in the evening, Jean spotted the mysterious couple emerge from the house and saunter arm-in-arm into the garden, the man still clutching his Gladstone bag. She waited anxiously for her husband, and at last he appeared.

'James, James,' whispered the wife, considerably agitated, 'I hope to God you didn't let that man take his bag round the rooms. I've been so worried – I thought he might knock you out with a spanner, and run off with the family jewellery.'

'But there's nothing wrong with the chap,' her husband contested breezily. 'He's got his own house open to the public; in fact, he was just telling me how they've had a lot of silver pinched recently, and how terrible it is that even treasure houses aren't safe any more. A perfectly respectable and decent man, my dear!'

'What house is this then?' Jean queried, deeply sceptical.

'Althorp, he says,' answered James, seemingly oblivious to the ramifications of such a statement.

Thus it was that Lord and Lady Spencer, parents of the royal bride-to-be, were mistaken for a pair of brigands, and the Starkies – particularly Jean – were left feeling very silly indeed.

She toyed with the idea of sending the story to the papers – 'Di's Father Taken for a Burglar!' – but considered on reflection that however good the publicity might be for Gaulden Manor, it probably wouldn't give the Spencers an awful lot of joy. How true – as it turned out, Lord Spencer got quite enough media coverage from unscrupulous tabloids to last him a lifetime, without the added difficulties of being labelled a roving kleptomaniac.

From the Hon. Gerald Maitland-Carew of Thirlestane Castle, in Berwickshire, seat of the Earls of Lauderdale

One afternoon, whilst going through our state dining room, a rather loud American ludicrously overdressed in tartan, latched on to me as though we were old pals.

As the tour progressed, he became increasingly familiar. This would've been fine had he not persisted in a line of banalities and ill-conceived assumptions about my family. Pointing to a portrait of the Duke of Lauderdale, painted by Sir Peter Lely in 1672, he grabbed me by the sleeve and said he could well see the family resemblance.

Exasperated by this final dose of pushiness, I replied that in his time the Duke was well known as the ugliest man in the kingdom. With that I made my escape.

Every stately home has a visitors' book. In theory, it gives people a chance to make comments on what they have seen and heard. In practice, it is an invitation for praise, raillery, or good old-fashioned abuse. This last seems to be perpetuated, in the main, by small children who see the book as the perfect opportunity to practise their doodles, and occasionally, their command of the English swear word. Adults tend to be more constructive though no less direct.

At one stage we only had the ground floor of Weston open to the public. This prompted the repeated entry, 'We want to see some bedrooms!'

Naturally, the following year we opened up two bedrooms. The reaction? 'We want to see more bedrooms!'

Paying heed to the request, we unlocked a few more, which elicited no further comment, so we must have got it about right.

This is where the visitors' book is most useful – ensuring

supply and demand. But it has entertainment value too. We especially enjoyed the wit of someone who wrote, 'Not bad for a two up, two down', and another who filled in the words 'Name: The Marquess of Sade; Address: Hell.'

And the guides have always taken one entry as a great personal compliment: 'Lovely house, nice guides, well preserved!'

Still, you the reader would like to know more about the raillery I suspect. A couple of examples will have to do.

Cawdor, commonly held as the most romantic castle in the Highlands, was opened to the public in 1976. Shortly after this someone on their first (and presumably last) trip to the famous fourteenth-century keep decided that the modest admission price was really far too high.

He made an acute historical observation in the visitors' book: 'If you had charged like this at the Battle of Culloden, you might have won!'

In the public showing visitors' book at St Osyth's Priory in Essex, Somerset de Chair has seen his home praised in many different ways – 'so peaceful', 'beautiful', 'fantastic, historic, and very well maintained'. But one day he came across, 'What a conceited and self-satisfied family they are!' Evidently a visitor had objected to the art collection which contains a host of family portraits, including two distinguished First Ministers – the Earl of Strafford, executed in 1641, and Lord Rockingham, Prime Minister before and after Lord North.

Somerset answers the charge succinctly: 'These items are listed for historic reasons, not out of family vanity.'

Castle Howard, an eighteenth-century palace designed by Sir John Vanbrugh in 1699, set between two lakes, is undoubtedly the finest private residence in Yorkshire, with a gilded dome that reaches 80 feet into the sky. It became famous when *Brideshead Revisited*, Evelyn Waugh's classic, was filmed there in the 1980s.

After touring the magnificent and impressive interior of Castle Howard, two slightly aged Yorkshire housewives, in their best summer print dresses, had returned to the north front. There they seated themselves on a convenient bench, from where they could admire the picturesque view over the great lake towards the Yorkshire moors in the far distance.

After sitting in contemplative silence for a few minutes, one turned to the other and said, 'What a grand view. I don't know about you, luv, but there's nothing inside that I'd want in my front room.'

The late George Howard – father of The Hon. Simon Howard, who now lives with his wife at Castle Howard and is responsible for its day-to-day operations – held many important public posts, including the chairmanship of the BBC. Like most people who have held that post, he was naturally rather well known, and one blunt local visitor to Castle Howard was heard to remark, 'Well I never, ain't life bloody marvellous, to think all this cums wit' chairmanship of BBC!'

Parnham is an Elizabethan Manor House in West Dorset, restored by Nash and surrounded by gardens landscaped by Inigo Thomas. The owners, John and Jennie Makepeace, are quite a duo. Jennie has extensively replanted the gardens over recent years, whilst John makes furniture in the workshop for public and private collections. Parnham has been hailed as a focal point for the renaissance in English furniture design.

During one of the open days, a lady visitor came out of the

famous furniture workshop, and seeing John, called him over. 'Tell me,' she asked gravely. 'Is Mr Makepeace still alive?'

John, at that time a young forty-five, managed to smile before answering, 'Just about, I think.'

But the stately home experience is clearly also an enervating one: In the woodland at Parnham there is a large assault net attached to the branch of an evergreen oak. In an adjacent tree hangs a long rope on which to swing.

One summer's afternoon, Jennie was sitting high up in the oak, having just lowered the net for repair. She was waiting for her son to bring her a ladder, when round the corner wandered a little old lady, dressed in regimental LOL costume – hat, woollen coat, glasses – and carrying a handbag.

Little old lady stops, looks longingly at the rope, glances around furtively, and begins to remove her outer garments which she places with her handbag against a neighbouring tree. Then she leaps to catch the dangling cord, and whooping for joy, has a jolly good swing. Back and forth she goes, watched by an invisible, and utterly apoplectic Mrs Makepeace.

At length, the old swinger jumped off her rope, and retrieving her hat, coat and shoes, became a little old lady again as she wobbled off the way she had come.

Ticket offices at stately homes face one major problem – OAPs. I don't mean to suggest that elderly folk pose a particular physical threat, merely that they sometimes forget the concessionary offers available to them. So we have to remind them, and run the risk of causing offence. 'Madam, you do realize that you qualify for a senior citizen pass?'

'Senior citizen pass? But I'm only fifty-two! How dare you!'

Nevertheless, the man in the ticket office at Berkeley Castle in Gloucestershire thought he was being especially tactful when he asked one mature couple: 'Would you by any chance be senior citizens?'

'No, we are French citizens!' came the indignant rejoinder.

Sometimes I have the feeling of being a fly on the wall, as people, unaware of my proximity, come out with revealing comments.

A rather poor, school of Sir Peter Lely, painting of Charles II used to hang at the top of the main staircase at Weston Park. My mother must have been in slightly mischievous mood when she put it there because on one side she positioned a portrait of Henrietta Maria, Charles's wife, and on the other, Moll Davis, one of his more famous mistresses!

I well remember observing a particular couple going round the house. The wife was voluble and extremely enthusiastic about everything, whilst the husband had clearly been dragged along to keep her company. He looked very bored indeed.

She had stopped in front of the portrait of Charles II for a considerable time, and the husband became increasingly frustrated. He was fiddling with his tie, then he began stamping his feet and muttering under his breath. Finally he could restrain himself no longer, and tried to yank his wife away from her protracted adorations.

An unusual tug of war began as she determinedly resisted his efforts. Suddenly, in the heat of the struggle, she cried out with great satisfaction: 'I can see what they saw in him now. I could really quite fancy him myself!'

Eastnor Castle in Herefordshire – described at the time of its completion as 'a princely and imposing pile', is the residence of James Hervey-Bathurst and his family.

One day James's father was loitering in a position to overhear quite easily the comments a visiting couple were making about the condition of the castle and its contents. The husband pointed out to his wife a gaping hole in one of the old carpets, and said, 'Don't you ever get at me again about the state of our carpets, this one's far worse.'

Bowood, the Georgian home of the Earl and Countess of Shelburne, is famed for its extensive gardens, some of which were landscaped by 'Capability' Brown.

A small boy – referring to the yew trees on the terrace – asked his mother, 'Why are those trees bent over?'

His mother replied, 'If you were two hundred years old, you'd be bent over.'

A German visitor, on being requested to refrain from using his video camera, asked if it was possible to film the notice which read, 'Please do not use video cameras in the house.'

A small girl asked in the Adam library, 'Please, miss, where do you get the book stamped if you want to borrow one?'

Two elderly spinsters to a security officer, 'We came here because you have the largest lawn in the country. Well, we have the smallest!'

In the centre of Warwick stands England's finest medieval castle, Warwick Castle, which was originally ordered to be built by William the Conqueror in 1068. Over the centuries, successive Earls added to the collection of armour, paintings and other *objets d'art* including personal belongings of Queen Elizabeth I, Queen Anne, and Marie Antoinette; in 1978 the castle was acquired by Madame Tussaud's who restored the eighteenth-century stables and the private apartments.

Today the castle is, perhaps, best known for the outstanding armoury and great hall where the enthusiast can pour over anything from cross-bows to one of Oliver Cromwell's own helmets and for its medieval dungeon, whose walls bear inscriptions by prisoners captured in the Civil War. Guests can even choose to have bed and breakfast in the dungeon, if they are that way inclined!

Some years ago, a Far Eastern crown prince came to see the dungeon for himself. Tall, distinguished and laconic, he arrived with a troupe of bodyguards who encircled the royal guest wherever he went, right hands stuck menacingly though totally unnecessarily under their left armpits as though about to draw a gun on an unseen would-be assassin.

The curator pointed to a set of wall-stocks, commenting, 'Dreadful things these, sir ... just imagine hanging upside down in them – for days on end!'

The Prince stopped in front of the instrument of torture, looked at it, then around him, and remarked with a sad, slight smile, 'Yes, but at least he could enjoy the excellence of the medieval architecture.'

The curator did not think it prudent to continue this particular line of conversation.

Another time a male visitor was so impressed with the look of an early eighteenth-century flintlock pistol that he called over a guide, pointed to the antique firearm, and asked imploringly, 'Oh come on – how much for the gun?'

But it is the plaster death masks of Oliver Cromwell, famous for their artistic realism, that have elicited most comment from the public. A middle-aged woman paused in front of a mask for some time before conjecturing, 'Dear me, looking at him I don't think he can have been feeling very well when that was taken.'

And an American, impressed with her own knowledge of the castle and its contents, was heard to say of the mask, 'Okay, that figures, but on what occasions might he perhaps have worn that?'

From Longleat House, family seat of the Marquess of Bath, designed for Sir John Thynne in 1580 and still lived in by his descendants. It was the first large Elizabethan house to be built in the Italian Renaissance style, and arguably the first stately home to be opened to the public, in 1949. In 1966 the late Lord Bath also launched the first drive-through wild animal reserve outside Africa.

A large American lady, with a substantial 'Tour of Britain' label plastered across her equally ample bosom, stated: 'We haven't got time to look at *anything*, honey. We just wanted to cross Longleat off our list.'

And another American inquired of one of the guides in the great hall: 'Is this where Lord Bath holds his balls and dances?'

One sunny day whilst standing on the front steps of Longleat House, a little grey-haired lady recognized a member of staff and informed him: 'Excuse me, I would just like to say what a lovely place you have here and that I've had a wonderful time, but have to admit to being a wee bit disappointed.'

The young man replied, 'I'm sorry to hear that. May I ask why?'

She sat down on the steps and sighed, 'I've been here all day, I've even had a picnic in the grounds, but I haven't seen a single lion walk past.'

He sat down beside her and inquired politely, 'Didn't you go round the safari park?'

She looked at him in astonishment and asked, 'The safari park? Where's that?'

From Alexander Thynn, Marquess of Bath

I have dwelt since 1953 in one corner of Longleat House, where the drawing room is not precisely at ground level, but half a storey up. That is to say that there is a basement storey whose windows are at knee-height when viewed from the outside, whereas the windows of my drawing room are supposedly too high up on the wall for anyone to peer in and see what might be going on inside. Or that is what I thought until the following incident occurred – way back in the 60s, I think it must have been.

I was seated in an armchair at the back of the drawing room when I perceived that there was the head of a man, totally unknown to me and just slightly older than myself, peering through the window at me. I was considerably surprised, since his action required that he should have pulled himself up on to the window ledge from the ground which was some ten feet below the ledge. I looked across the room at him with unconcealed displeasure in my expression, supposing that this would instigate his immediate retreat. But the face did not budge an inch. So I reinforced the signal I was sending him by rising slowly from my chair – still to no effect. I then felt required to move towards him, with my anger now tinged with menace. My pace was slow, but he was still clinging to the window sill by the time that I reached the window pane, which was all that now separated us.

I had really given no thought to the contingencies of how this situation might develop, in the event of the intruder persisting with his offensive behaviour. There we were, glaring at one another with just the thickness of the glass between us. But it occurred to me that I ought to be saying something. So I mimed the part, as if there were some words emerging from my mouth – impossible for him to hear perhaps, but to be imagined in bubble captions which he could then read. After a moment's hesitation, however, he responded in a similar vein, opening and shutting his mouth as if effectively answering me back.

It was thus that we continued, for prolonged seconds. But the longer the situation had to be endured, the more it worked in my favour, for the simple reason that (hanging there from a window ledge without his feet touching the ground) his posture must have been physically uncomfortable. In any case, he did eventually drop back to the ground, shuffling off with a few more scowls thrown over his shoulder in my direction. He was leaving me in territorial possession of the window pane, but with the idea that I might count on privacy within my own drawing room now shattered.

It was perhaps at this moment that the idea first took place in my mind that, one day, I might have to shift my private suite of rooms up to the top floor at Longleat, where it would take a far more courageous intruder to scale the wall so as to examine me through a far higher drawing room window. It is a move which I have at last now made, and it furnishes me with a vantage point from which I can still be seen peering out at the tourists who are so precious to a stately home's economy. But the closer inspection of both myself and of my innermost sanctum can only be obtained by invitation.

Breamore – home of Sir Westrow Hulse, Bt

An aged couple, buying a ticket to go round the house, asked for, 'Two ancient Britons, please.'

A visitor remarked to his wife on seeing the gratuity box labelled 'Guides' at the exit door, 'Oh look, how nice, they're collecting for the Girl Guides.'

Breamore is noted for not being the warmest of houses. On a particularly cold day in April 1993, a middle-aged lady was overheard saying to her friend, 'I normally get hot flushes in these houses. I certainly won't need to worry about that here.'

A party of girls from a prestigious ladies college was being shown round Weston on a specially organized tour as part of their fine art appreciation course. They reached the dining room, and the guide began to describe some of the more valuable and important paintings that hang there.

'Over on this side is a portrait of Sir Thomas Hamner, which was exhibited at the Treasure Houses of Britain Exhibition in Washington. This picture, as well as four of the others here, was painted by Van Dyck of whom I'm sure you have heard.'

'Oh yes,' replied an enthusiastic pupil, 'I've seen his show on television!'

From Stratfield Saye – given by a grateful nation in 1817 to the Duke of Wellington after the defeat of Napoleon, and still the family home

Visitor in the Lady Charles room, 'The pictures are lovely – are they hand painted?'

A teacher, in sole charge of a group of schoolchildren, asked a steward, 'Who was the Duke of Wellington?'·

A visitor wondered whether, when the first Duke was in Parliament, he had a government car to bring him to Stratfield Saye each evening, as it was so far from London.

A belligerent gentleman in the front hall pompously asked, 'Right then – where's his armour?' He was told that the Duke of Wellington didn't wear armour, but responded, 'Why not? Henry the Eighth did!'

Far too often, people seem to be much more interested in demanding information than listening to the answers. One particular visitor had virtually interrogated a steward with a whole host of questions, but had apparently taken in none of the responses. In due course, he asked, 'Why did the Duke choose the middle of June for the battle?'

The steward, who by this time was becoming really rather exasperated, answered, 'He probably had to fit it in between Henley and Wimbledon.' To which the visitor, who had quite obviously not been listening at all, answered, 'Oh really,' and continued his tour of the house.

Most stately art collections seem to have come to an abrupt halt around the end of the eighteenth century. The reason for this, I suspect, lies somewhere between a decline in aristocratic spending power and a simple lack of wall space. But at Chatsworth House, which has an abundance of walls, the present Duke and Duchess of Devonshire have patronized some very famous modern artists.

The Duchess had her portrait painted by Lucien Freud, an artist whose style is certainly unique – some would describe it as gloomy even. As she says herself, 'The one of me was on the public route of the house for a time. Someone heard an old lady say to her friend, "That's the Dowager Duchess. It was taken the year she died." I was thirty-four when it was painted, but the old lady had a point; the face is sadly raddled, and a pale green moustache covers the upper lip. There is no doubt that I get more like the painting every year.'

The picture has been moved to a less conspicuous position in the private part of the house, where it can no longer be viewed by the public.

Not many homes are fortunate enough to have a safari park attached. However in May 1970, the Duke of Bedford created the one at Woburn, within the 3,000-acre deer park surrounding the house. Both the wildlife and the Abbey, built on the site of a twelfth-century Cistercian monastery, attract thousands of visitors a year.

They also attract telephone pranksters. The switchboard is regularly afflicted with callers keen to get through to a 'Mr C. Lion, please', 'Mr G. Raffe', or 'Miss Elly Phant, if she's available'. What is surprising, the Woburn staff tell me, is that each of these comic genii believes him or herself to be the originator of the jokes. (This is doubly sad, when you think about it. It's one thing peddling worn-out clichés, quite another to admit to inventing them.) Needless to say, there's never a dull moment in the offices at Woburn. Only recently they had a mysterious request for 'Theresa Green, living in the park'. Think about it ... but not too hard.

The family and animals mix on equal terms. Lord and Lady Tavistock's youngest son, Lord James, was brought up with a tiger cub called Tiga. Rejected at birth by her mother, Tiga lived at Woburn for the first three months of her life where she was bottle fed in the nursery by a concerned Lady Tavistock, whilst Jamie slept in his cot.

After the family had enjoyed lunch at a friend's cottage near Henley one memorable Sunday, a three-year-old Jamie took the host by the hand and asked him, 'Please will you take me to see your lions now.' He thought that everybody had a safari park at the bottom of their garden.

As the years went by, Jamie became familiar with all the animals in the safari park, and spent many hours with them and their keepers. Growing up at Woburn might have turned any young boy into the most obsessive of amateur zoologists, but Jamie has always found time for more conventional adolescent activities. On more than one occasion Lady Tavistock has been confronted by a very irate head cleaner complaining about the marks on her freshly polished floors. But to Jamie, the Abbey has always been just home, and the long corridors and the expanse of the west hall perfect for practising his skate-boarding technique!

Noel Boxall, owner of Bickleigh Castle in Devon, watched as two elderly ladies took their time pottering round his home. When they came to the dining room, one old dear turned to the other and asked her, 'Do you think this place is still lived in?'

Her companion replied with absolute authority that this was certainly the case. The first lady inquired as to how she could be so sure. 'It must be lived in,' said the second impressively, 'because that silver bowl over there's got sugar in it!'

A full-length picture by Coypel of *Susannah at her Bath* hangs in the dining room at Weston Park. She has a magnificent, Junoesque figure and is almost completely nude – except for a small wisp of cloth which falls across her body in a conveniently strategic position.

A guide was taking a party of very young schoolchildren through the dining room, and was about to leave for the Marble Hall, when one little girl stopped right in front of the picture and stared up at it. Struck with horror, she blushed, hid her face in her hands, and rushed up to the guide, crying, 'Miss, Miss, that lady's got no knickers on!'

At Weston Park you will find little gravestones up against various walls in the garden. They mark the resting places of favourite family pets, which have been commemorated in this special way, with their names engraved for all to see.

My grandfather was very fond of his animals, a tribe of Pekingese dogs that followed him everywhere, nipping at the heels of gardeners and others who were foolish enough to impede their progress. Needless to say, the staff gave voice to appropriate words of parting at their respective funerals.

Some years ago, the owner of a well-known stately home in Yorkshire buried a beloved, favourite Labrador in his garden and put up a stone with its name on. The first day after the burial, two Yorkshire ladies came roaming through the grounds and stopped by the grave, as the owner stood by.

One of the ladies said to the other, 'Must be a gardener, I s'pose.'

'Yes, madam,' offered the owner mischievously. 'We work them so hard, we bury them where they drop.'

'Oh!' exclaimed the ladies in unison, and hurried away.

The following letter was received by The Earl of Shelburne at Bowood House in 1993.

Dear Sir/Madam,
Last year when our large family visited – things got lost and found again. But, unfortunately my lower dentures was not one of them.

One of the places we visited was your lovely house and restaurant and I wondered if I might have misled (*sic*) them after lunch and left them on the basin in the ladies' room.

If you have any could you let me know please. They had 1–3 teeth each end joined by a metal band.
Yours sincerely,

Alas, they did not turn up.

A nother letter received by the Earl of Shelburne drew to his attention the obvious shortcomings of Bowood and the family that lives there.

Whilst it is uncommon for stately homes to get such scorching correspondence, the compiler is keen to show all sides of the argument: historic houses, bastions of capitalist greed, or country retreats preserved for the benefit of the nation? Also, it has been thought necessary to include the letter on the grounds that it is very amusing.

Earl Shelburne (*sic*),
Bowood,
Wiltshire.

Dear Earl,

Could I suggest you get rid of Floris perfumes in favour of Cosmetics to Go which are vegetarian and sometimes vegan. Floris tend to be expensive, whereas the latter are fun and not expensive. Cosmetics to Go can be contacted on 0800 373 366.

Also I notice in your brochure that your family were up and coming from 1622. Bully for you. What most of the population of that period were not is 'up and coming'. So why do the masses now have to support the family home of those who couldn't care less for the lower orders?

Ashley Keithton (fictional name)

P.S. £4.00 to wander the grounds is excessive and just to go through a few old rooms is poor. Frankly, Sir, it is not good enough.

Thanks must go to the Earl for contributing this masterly critique of his home. Such openness is surely to his credit.

A handful of stories from Blenheim, home of the 11th Duke of Marlborough, and birthplace of Sir Winston Churchill

The Palace was built for John Churchill, 1st Duke of Marlborough, after his magnificent victory at the Battle of Blenheim in 1704; the land and £240,000 were given by Queen Anne and a grateful nation. But an American visitor once asked, 'Tell me, why did that French King give this palace to the Duke?'

A young Frenchman with his arm around an attractive Oriental girl asked a guide, 'Excuse me, but are you allowed to go upstairs here?'

An Indian visitor whispered to his friend, 'Just who was this Mr Blenheim?'

An enthusiastic Japanese tourist walked up to a guide before the start of the tour. 'Marlborough – he live here, yes?'
    'Yes, sir, that's correct.'
    'He make cigarettes, yes?'

Guide to a Libyan visitor, 'I'm afraid I cannot speak Arabic.'
    The Libyan visitor replied curtly, 'You will one day.'

A visitor once stepped inside the main entrance and asked, 'Excuse me. Can anyone tell me the name of this place?'

A small child, looking in awe at a model of the late Duke as a baby, inquired nervously: 'Was he really black?'
    An American looking at the same bronze piece commented, 'I know people who've had their shoes done, but this is the first time I've heard of bronzing the baby.'

A plain-speaking old age pensioner from Portsmouth, on hearing that Duchess Anne had eighteen children, remarked, 'She should have taken the pill, then.'

A visitor gazing at the Blenheim Tapestry asked the guide, 'How long did you say it took to paint this?'

Closing up a stately home after a long, hot summer's day is no laughing matter. Visitors, as a rule, like to linger. We have to tread a careful line between appearing inhospitable and the needs of security.

I certainly have no problem with those who want to tarry a little while, even two or three hours, after the official closing time of 5 o'clock. But there is no means of escape once the gates are locked and as much as visitors may appreciate the dusk at Weston, I'm not sure they'd really want to spend the night in the garden.

Occasionally I am forced to drive around the park in my car, staring meaningfully out of the window in an attempt to shift dawdling parties. But this is rare and I don't like having to do it. Visitors have come to visit after all, not to be stared at by me.

I remember once being forced to 'evict' a group of Indian visitors, who had crept through the gates two hours after closure and taken up various picnicking positions in front of the house. They seemed keen to stay on well into the night, which would have been fine if they'd booked, or at least paid an entrance fee, but they had done neither. I had to cross swords with them, so to speak, and when I eventually got home, told my family about the encounter.

One of my young sons, who had that evening been glued to a John Wayne film on television, raised his eyebrows in surprise and admiration when I told my wife about the incident. 'Daddy, have you really had a fight with the Red Indians?' he spluttered. 'Cor, you're brave! Did they have bows and arrows?'

It didn't seem fair to shatter his illusions about the dangers of running a stately home. And besides, it's quite nice to be acknowledged as a hero once in a while.

Charles Clive-Ponsonby-Fane tells a horror story on the same subject

I have a dog called Bunford. I always take him with me when I lock up at the end of the day. At times, when a party is tarrying awhile before going home, the sight of a bouncy black Labrador lolloping determinedly towards them has proved enough to drive even the most steadfast back to their cars, and down the drive.

Late one evening, whilst doing my final rounds, I noticed a red Morris 1100 in the car park. A man and his wife were lounging in the car, and with granny reclining in a deck-chair just beside them, all three looked utterly satisfied as they sipped tea, munched through their sandwiches, and basked in the warmth of the setting sun. Sadly their idyll was relatively short-lived; Bunford got one sniff of granny's snack, and he was off.

Bounding across the gravel, he came upon granny, gave her a quick, loving lick – which I'm not sure she appreciated – and took a large bite from her sandwich. I watched with alarm as he consumed the morsel in one gulp, then switched his attention to a whole box of sandwiches which were resting on the front seat of the car. In one leap, he was on to granny's lap, into the vehicle, and at the tuckbox.

Pandemonium. Mother screams, father's tea goes all over

his trousers, and granny, well granny does the strangest thing. Moving like a three-year-old, she jumps from the deck-chair, scoots round the car and gets into the back seat on the other side. Once ensconced she slams the door and locks it.

A somewhat melodramatic action this, for it has exactly the opposite effect to the one she intended. Bunford was now safely secured in the car, and happy to set about the large number of tupperware boxes piled high on the back seat.

He went through them like a whirlwind – and granny became very agitated indeed. Still, she might have saved herself considerable trouble if she had relinquished her hold on the remains of the original sandwich. As she waved her arms about in confused panic, it all seemed to Bunford like some amusing game – he clambered and slobbered over the poor woman, occasionally snapping at the elusive tit-bit.

Meantime mother is still screaming. I'm shouting at granny to open the door, granny's howling at the dog to leave her alone, and the dog, not to be outdone, starts barking. Father, God bless him, is out of the car, splitting his sides with laughter.

At length, I manage to liberate Bunford from the back seat. The husband, grinning from ear to ear, comes up and puts his arm around my shoulder. 'I like thee pup,' he said, in a thick Yorkshire accent. 'He's a grand chap. Taken quite a fancy to the mother-in-law!' With that, he emits a hearty guffaw, and patting Bunford affectionately on the head, hops back into his car to pacify two very traumatized relations. He had his work cut out!

⚜